# Free Motion Quilting Handbook

A Machine Quilting Beginners Guide for Learning How to Quilt Free Motion Designs on Modern Projects Plus Tips, Tools, and Techniques Included

By

Zera Meyer

Copyright © 2022 – Zera Meyer

All rights reserved

No part of this publication may be reproduced, distributed, or transmitted in any form or by any means, including photocopying, recording, or other electronic or mechanical methods, without the prior written permission of the publisher, except in the case of brief quotations embodied in reviews and certain other non-commercial uses permitted by copyright law.

## Disclaimer

This publication is designed to provide competent and reliable information regarding the subject matter covered. However, the views expressed in this publication are those of the author alone, and should not be taken as expert instruction or professional advice. The reader is responsible for his or her own actions.

The author hereby disclaims any responsibility or liability whatsoever that is incurred from the use or application of the contents of this publication by the purchaser or reader. The purchaser or reader is hereby responsible for his or her own actions.

# Table of Contents

Introduction .................................................................................. 6

Chapter 1 ..................................................................................... 8

Free-Motion Quilting Fundamentals ...................................... 8

    Free-Motion Quilting – What Is It About? ...................... 8

    Drawback of Free-Motion Quilting .................................. 9

    Advantages of Free-Motion Quilting ............................. 10

    The Popularity of Free-Motion Quilting ....................... 11

Chapter 2 ................................................................................... 12

Tips and Tricks In Free-Motion Quilting .............................. 12

Chapter 3 ................................................................................... 19

Terms and Definitions In Free-Motion Quilting ................. 19

    Quilt Top Terms ............................................................... 19

    Quilting Design Terms .................................................... 20

    Machine Quilting Terms ................................................. 22

Chapter 4 ................................................................................... 26

Getting Started With Free-Motion Quilting ........................... 26

  Tools and Materials ................................................................ 26

    Sewing Machine ................................................................ 26
    Extension Table ................................................................. 29
    Fabric ................................................................................... 30
    Thread ................................................................................. 32
    Needles ............................................................................... 35
    Batting ................................................................................. 35
    Marking Tools .................................................................... 37
    Pen and Paper .................................................................... 38
    Quilting Rulers .................................................................. 39
    Basting Pins ........................................................................ 40
    Scissors ................................................................................ 41
    Quilting Gloves ................................................................. 42
    Supreme Sliders ................................................................. 43
    Free-Motion Machine Foot .............................................. 44

  Setting Up Your Quilting Workarea .................................... 46

  Getting Your Machine Up and Ready ................................ 51

  Practicing Your Free-Motion Quilting On Paper ............. 54

  Popular Designs In Free-Motion Quilting ......................... 56

    Loops ................................................................................... 56
    Pebbles, Bubbles, Pearls ................................................... 60
    Meander and Stipple ........................................................ 65
    Paisley ................................................................................. 68

- Teardrops ............................................................................ 70
- Feathers ............................................................................... 72
- Swirls .................................................................................. 72
- Geometric ........................................................................... 73
- Vining Leaves .................................................................... 74
- Vining Flowers .................................................................. 75

Chapter 5 ........................................................................................ 77

Free-Motion Quilting Projects ................................................... 77

    Quilted Placemats ................................................................ 77

    Quilted Potholder ................................................................. 88

    Quilted Coasters ................................................................. 104

    Quilted Table Runner ....................................................... 118

Chapter 6 ...................................................................................... 134

Troubleshooting Free-Motion Quilting Issues ...................... 134

Conclusion ................................................................................... 140

# Introduction

Quilting is an art that involves the binding of three layers—the quilt top, the batting, and the backing material—to form a single piece that can be used as an embellishment, wall hanging, or for the provision of warmth. This craft takes the art of sewing to a deeper level, where you also get to work with a machine called a quilting machine.

Now, the term 'free-motion quilting' describes a technique by which you could finish your quilted projects. You get to quilt lines and other curves just to design the surface of your project too. Many a time, most quilters just get confused as to the design to work with and would just spend hours hooping over their machine, trying to figure out something.

In this quilting art, you get to exercise your brain and creativity in ways you wouldn't have thought possible. That is why the technique of drawing out your design before you begin your Free-motion quilting is a very great way to start off. That way, your hands can get used to the pattern or design you intend to quilt.

Now, regardless of whether you can draw or not, you can still undertake this art brilliantly. The technique of drawing on paper is simply to get your rain accustomed to whatever design you are making. That way, you'd find it easier to go ahead with the actual free-motion quilting on fabric.

You also shouldn't worry too much about imperfect quilts when you start quilting. It gets better as you continue. In this book, several tips will be discussed to get you quilting the right way. Most importantly, ensure you enjoy every moment of the free-motion quilting experience.

Now, let's take a deep dive into the art of free-motion quilting.

# Chapter 1

# Free-Motion Quilting Fundamentals

**Free-Motion Quilting – What Is It About?**

Free-motion quilting is a type of machine quilting that can be done on a domestic machine or a long arm quilting machine. The darning foot, a unique foot made to hover over your quilt's surface and allow you to move the quilt in all directions, is used to Free-motion quilt.

You can make great designs and patterns on your quilt's surface by moving in all directions.

The quilt top, batting, and backing in Free-motion quilting, are quilted without using the feed-dogs in moving the sandwiched quilts forward.

In free-motion quilting, the stitches' size is determined by the machine's speed and the movements of the quilter's hand, rather than by the machine, as is the case with traditional machine sewing with feed dogs. Quilting can be done with a stencil or a pre-drawn line, or it can be done free-hand without the need for a drawn pattern.

## Drawback of Free-Motion Quilting

The free-motion style of quilting is rather a peculiar type of quilting, and one issue that most people find with it is its technique. The term 'Free-motion' means that you'd be free to move your project in whatever direction you please—forward, backward, or any other way you desire. However, even though that little freedom sounds pleasant, it cancels out the usage of feed dogs.

Feed dogs are tiny projections that are situated beneath the presser foot of your machine. To work with them, all you'd need to do is run the ends of your project through the space between the projections. As you run the ends of your project forward, you'd be able to notice symmetrical and evenly spaced seams.

So, yes, you not being able to use your feed dogs means that you'd have to figure out how to make your seams spaced evenly. And that is where most of the challenges with free-motion quilting lies. So, to solve this issue, you would have to work on keeping your hands balanced and stable as you push the quilt towards the needles. Also, the feet sitting on the feet pedal of the quilting machine should be balanced so that the speed can be correctly regulated.

These balance strategies and moves make the art of free quilting seem quite difficult for beginners. Most times, instead of projects with evenly spaced stitches, you'd end up seeing projects with stitches that are mainly asymmetrical. This quilting style also creates a situation where you are responsible for the direction towards which the feed moves, the design you end up with, and the speed at which the machine moves – all of this could be very overwhelming for a beginner.

**Advantages of Free-Motion Quilting**

Aside from ensuring the seams are even and straight or that the machine is being operated at the correct speed rate, there are still a few benefits attached to this art. Some of them include the following;

1. Free-motion quilting may be used to quilt intricate motifs. Curving designs are feasible because you can move the quilt in all directions, sideways, and from the front to back, without being turned.
2. Effortless quilting without the feed dogs in Free-motion quilting can be achieved than quilting with them. In "stitch in the ditch" or straight-line

grid quilting, a quilter can wander over the quilt's surface without needing to follow a line.
3. Free-motion quilting enhances the quilt's beauty while also allowing you to finish quilt tops much more quickly than hand quilting.

## The Popularity of Free-Motion Quilting

You might still be wondering what really makes free-motion quilting unique and popular amongst quilters. Well, here are a couple of reasons;

1. Free-motion quilting requires no additional equipment and offers endless creative possibilities. Any sewing machine in good functioning condition can be used for free-motion quilting.
2. Free-motion quilting allows you to create incredibly complicated motifs without the need to rotate the quilt since you control the movement's direction and speed.
3. Free-motion quilting lets you express your quilting style, whether you choose conventional

motifs like feathers or more humorous motifs like Sailboats and Sewing Scissors.

## Chapter 2

## Tips and Tricks In Free-Motion Quilting

To be successful in free-motion quilting, you must be familiar with the tips and tricks of the art, or perhaps you are looking for a way to add stunning machine quilting texture to your quilts but don't know what to do? This section will address your needs.

**1. Get a wide table surface area for your quiltings**

The best surfaces you should use for your quilting projects are the entirely smooth surfaces—not floors. The weight of your quilt will be pulled down by gravity, causing it to drag and create friction, which will prevent the forming of excellent stitches. Drag can be avoided by lifting the quilt off the floor and placing it on a table. Utilize the widest tabletop surface you can find and set up portable tables around you to keep the bulk under control as much as you can.

## 2. Match the top and bobbin thread colors

When threading your machine, pay attention to the thread you use. You may see spots of bobbin thread showing through on your quilt's top or the thread of your needle popping through on the backside if your tension isn't correct. Use a matching color of thread in your machine's top and bobbin to avoid this. They don't have to be the same weight or fiber content, but matching colors will keep those little "popups" hidden!

## 3. Hide your errors by working with thin threads that blends and fabric prints that are busy

When you choose multicolored fabric prints that appear to be "busy," the texture of your quilting will stand out more than any imperfections in your stitching. For machine quilting, use a thin (50 weight or a little less) polyester thread or cotton in a color that matches your quilt top. This keeps your quilt from looking "thready" and hides all kinds of errors!

## 4. Run several practice sessions with scraps and small projects

It's tempting to get right in and start working on a big quilt right away. However, just as you should practice cutting and sewing before making your first quilt top, free-motion quilting also requires practice.

Make some practice samples by layering two 10 inches or larger fabric scraps with batting in between. You can experiment with different combinations of thread, test some batting types, inspect your tension, and stitch some designs to see how they turn out. Keep these samples as a guide, taking notes as you go. Once you're satisfied with your efforts, go ahead and make smaller projects, e.g., potholder, table runner, or baby quilt, before moving onto bigger projects.

## 5. Ensure you make your quilts yourself

Many quilters spend several time piecing but then hire someone else to sew their quilts, and they never get used to the machine quilting process. Making quilts yourself from the start will make your machine quilting skills at par with your piecing skills, and you will be able to enhance both skills as you progress.

6. **Start with the basic quilting designs**

Choose a simple quilting design to complement your first quilt. For example, quilting with a walking foot using straight lines or a free-motion foot in an allover stipple or swirly design can be achieved successfully.

> When sewing charm quilts, I prefer to utilize a method I call "stitch near the ditch." I use a blending thread and a decorative stitch on my machine to quilt over the seam lines. It's a quick technique to quilt, and it doesn't have to be flawless to look good. If I want to add extra quilting later, I can always go back in and do so.

7. **Draft out a plan for your quilting before you jump right into it**

> I like to photograph my quilt tops or use quilt design software to sketch them out on the computer (such as Electric Quilt). Before I begin quilting, I draw my quilting designs on printed paper. This gives me the opportunity to "interview" designs and evaluate how they will work with the pieced top. It also assists me in

determining where I should travel across the quilt during quilting.

8. **Ensure that the background of your project has lots of texture**

   Contrary to common opinion, some of the most complex-looking free-motion quilting motifs are actually the simplest to create. Variety and asymmetry are the keys to creating a stunning backdrop texture. Stencils and washable marking tools can be used to position crucial parts of your quilting design, then thick background quilting in a range of sizes can be used to fill in the gaps around them.

9. **Ensure you maintain the right posture**

   Maintain adequate ergonomics and healthy posture. If you position yourself for success, you will get great results and skip a visit to the chiropractor. Your laps should be in a parallel position to your arms and hands and comfortably rest on the sewing machine's bed. Relax by lowering your shoulders.

10. **Ensure you work with proper lighting**

Your entire body is strained as a result of eye strain. Ensure your quilt and workspace are properly illuminated. When I quilt, I position the fixture of my light behind me so that the light shines straight above my shoulder and beneath the needle.

11. **First, draw the design**

    Drawing a design with a pen and paper without lifting the pen means you can probably quilt as well. Every day, keep a notepad close by and doodle a few designs. You will improve as you draw more designs. Drawing is a great way to stimulate your creative juice, much like practicing on your machine.

12. **Mind your feet**

    Open-toed, clear, hopping, or closed? They are all effective; you simply have to pick the best one for the job. For the majority of my free-motion quilting, I use a transparent plastic foot, but I have numerous possibilities. The trick is to figure out what works best for you. Make an appointment with your machine dealer and inquire about testing them all out before buying.

# Chapter 3

# Terms and Definitions In Free-Motion Quilting

Several terminologies are used when working with free-motion of quilting. These terms and their definitions would help you become even more familiar with the art of free-motion quilting. They include the following;

**Quilt Top Terms**
- Block: This is a term that describes a small portion of a quilt top project that can either be ordinary fabric or a series of patched projects.
- Borders: This is a term that describes the strips of fabric used to surround the central square of a quilted piece.
- Focus fabric: This term describes printed fabric that ranges from medium to big-sized fabric. The focus fabric can be any color of your choice.
- Layout: This term describes how the blocks and borders are arranged in your quilting projects.
- Quilt bundle: This bundle comprises the top, batting, and backing piece.

- Setting triangles: These triangles of fabric are usually used for filling up the edges, corners, and spaces left after the blocks have been set.

**Quilting Design Terms**
- Continuous object designs: This term defines a quilting design with interlocking rows of motifs seamed with one string of thread.
- Corner block: This is a square-shaped design that lines the edges of the borders of your project.
- Fill patterns: This term describes a style of quilting where different patterns are used to fill the background of your art in a particular pattern.
- Formal: This term describes the precise quilting of curves or straight lines
- Free-form: This is a technique used to fill a background pattern with your hand as a guide. Your hand follows the pattern in your head. However, what you craft out could be of any size. This free-form could also help guide the quilting machine without using an actual pattern.

- Grids: This term describes straight lines that form patterns like squares or diamonds when they are stitched.
- Long arm: This term describes a kind of quilting machine with the head-mounted on a mobile rack that makes its move through quilt tops fixed to rollers.
- Meandering: This term defines a bigger and better version of stippling
- Motif: This term is used to describe the template that is used for quilting projects
- Navigation: This term is used to describe the sequence that is followed when quilting out a project.
- Retrace: This is when seam lines are doubled by threading through them again.
- Seam line: This is a line that helps attach the patchwork to the borders.
- Stitchable design: This phrase explains the drawing of simple image outlines using stitch lines.

- Stitch in the ditch: This term is used to describe the art of quilting right into stitch lines, to attach two or more layers with the aid of the walking foot and feed dogs. It could also be done with the aid of free-motion quilting.
- Stippling: This term represents a background fill pattern that comprises curves and continuous lines of seams that fill the background with quilted motif designs.

**Machine Quilting Terms**
- Feed dogs: This term refers to the metal teeth beneath the stitch plate that moves the fabric or quilted material.
- Free-hand: This term refers to quilting designs that are created when the machine is guided with the hand. Here, you do not have to follow lines or marks. The pattern you follow usually is in your mind.
- Follow-the-line machine quilting: This term is used when a quilting design that is either straight

or curved is marked on the quilt and followed with either a walking foot or free-motion quilting.
- Hand-guided free-motion: This term is used when following a marked line or making stitch-free patterns in the quilter's memory.
- Jump stitch: This term is used to travel from a motif to another detached position on the quilt. First, you'd need to stitch the first motif and lock the stitches. Then, you'd lift the pressure foot to release the bobbin thread's tension. Once that is done, slide the bundle to the location where you desire to lock the threads for sewing. The long top and bobbin threads are usually cut short to prevent a scenario where they are overstretched.
- Home and domestic: These terms are interchangeable and refer to the normal sewing machine.
- Locking stitches: This term describes the process of fastening the beginning and the end of a stitch line by grouping six to seven stitches closely.
- Refined free-motion quilting: This term describes the art of working with the free-motion quilting

technique with a refined focus. Then, intricate quilting designs are made with lightweight thread.
- Stitch-in-the-ditch quilting: As described above.
- Stippling: As described above.
- Walking foot: This tool is an attachment used with a sewing machine to replace the presser foot. It works with the feed dogs to move the several layers of fabric together. Here, you must note that the feed dogs can help the bundle move in different directions when engaged. The stitch length setting can also be adjusted to determine the stitch length.

## A Short Message From The Author:

Hey, I hope you are enjoying the book? I would love to hear your thoughts!

Many readers do not know how hard reviews are to come by and how much they help an author.

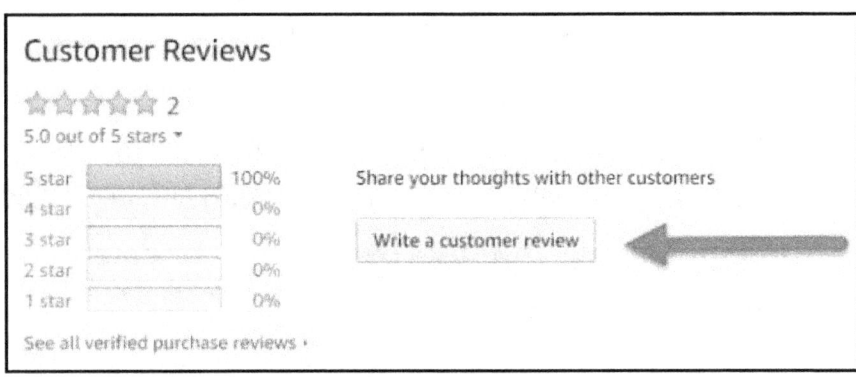

I would be incredibly grateful if you could take just 60 seconds to write a short review on Amazon, even if it is a few sentences!

\>> Click here to leave a quick review

Thanks for the time taken to share your thoughts!

# Chapter 4

# Getting Started With Free-Motion Quilting

**Tools and Materials**

When working with the free-motion quilting technique, you are going to need a couple of tools and supplies, which include the following;

**Sewing Machine**

The kind of sewing machine you get should fit well with your free-motion quilting objective. This machine usually works for quilting patterns, sketching designs on fabric, or painting a square of fabric with a thread string, among others. Now, there are different types of sewing machines you'd find out there. One is the Domestic sewing machine. The other type is the Long-arm sewing machine.

But first, let's take a look at the features you should look out for when choosing any sewing machine, be it domestic or long arm;

- A machine whose feed drop can be dropped

- A sewing machine to which a lighting system can be fixed (This will ensure that you have enough visibility as you work on your project)
- A machine with the ability to fit in a Free-motion foot
- A machine that can stitch the usual straight stitches and stitches of the zigzag style.
- A machine with an open-toe foot
- A machine with a flatbed extension table for extra quilting space (needed when quilting large projects
- A knee lift
- A machine that
- Needle Up/Down
- Easy tension adjuster
- Controls for width and length of stitches
- A machine that can make great curves and decorative stitches

Also, a machine with several computerized parts may not be too suitable for free-motion quilting. That is because it could take very long moments to make the necessary adjustments. That is why you should always ensure that you practice with a sewing machine before you finally purchase it. You also want to ensure that you like the darning foot.

Now, let's move onto the differences between the two types of machines from which you can decide which is best to opt for.

| Long-arm sewing machine | Domestic sewing machine |
|---|---|
| The size of the throat is very large compared to that of the domestic sewing machine—about 20 inches. | The throat size is smaller in the domestic sewing machine—about eight inches. |
| This machine allows the quilt being worked on to move very freely, which is a feature great for free-motion quilting. | This machine doesn't allow random movement of the fabric. |
| You can work freely on your quilts without having to shift your hands too many times. This feature makes it very suitable for curves and other intricate designs. | You cannot work without having to move your hands. This feature makes it unsuitable for free-motion quilting involving curves and other intricate designs. |
| It has a motor that can work quickly, i.e., by producing thousands of stitches within a minute | The motor is not as strong as that of the long-arm sewing machine |
| The long-arm sewing machine is oriented sideways so that you can move your quilt easily without it getting in the way. | The domestic sewing machine usually faces you, and so, as you move the fabric towards the throat of the machine, you'd find it getting in your way. |

## Extension Table

This table is required to complement your sewing machine. Sewing machines do not necessarily have a wide workspace to place your quilted project on.

Quilted projects are usually larger, so the extension table is what you need to fix to your machine to increase your workspace.

Although some sewing machines come with these extension tables, however, if your sewing machine does not come with an extension table, then it's best to get one of these, and you can easily fix the table to your machine when you need to, and then, have it unhinged after usage. That way, you'd be able to move your quilt about more easily as you work it towards the needle.

**Fabric**

Without this material, you can pretty much do nothing. First, you'd have to work with a fabric of very high quality. You'd also want to work with a type of fabric that you can easily set in a place without it moving about. That usually defines the stability of the fabric. One fabric that settles all these requirements is the quilter's cotton. Materials like silk, satin, and velvet have quite slippery surfaces and would end up sliding across your work table if you ever work with them.

Solid foundation fabric would be highly useful when you have to sketch or paint a design using thread. You could choose to work with fabrics that have a patterned background or a simple, bold background. Beginners might want to consider using solid colors as backgrounds first before moving on to the other types. Also, the purchase of cuts like the fat quarters allows you to choose the color you need for the background of your project. That way, you can work without having to buy several yards of fabric.

Fabric is also a very ubiquitous commodity. You could buy in-store or online, but you should always look out for quality. The quality of fabric increases with its thread count. The ones with a high thread count are usually referred to as those with high quality and vice versa. Thread count is a term that is determined by counting the number of thread lines that lie horizontally and vertically within a square inch.

High-quality fabric usually turns out to be the best for quilting art and thread painting.

**Thread**

Thread is another very important material in quilting art. As a quilter, it would be more than adequate if you had several colors and types of thread that you could work with when making a project. All you need to do when starting is to pick out the type of thread you want to work with. You would notice that the common thread types are the ones that are made from rayon, polyester, or cotton.

Threads made from polyester and rayon usually give your project a glossy and bright appearance, while those made from cotton give your project a matted appearance. So, you should go for whichever look would suit your project the most. Each of the materials used for thread production has its respective drawbacks and advantages. It is only up to you to decide which one you can maximize the best.

Once you cross the hurdle of thread selection, you'd then need to move over to selecting the weight of the thread you need. The weight is usually indicated on the reel. The higher the number you see, the lesser the weight. Also, the lesser the weight, the finer it is for use. For free-motion quilting, you would want to use very light thread strings. For example, a sample of polyester with a weight of 40g would work better for quilting than that of a 50g thread.

You'd also need to pick out the color you need. When you need the color of the thread to pop out on your project, you should ensure that the color contrasts sharply with the color of the fabric you use. However, if you want to keep the thread out of view, you could go for ones with colors that match the fabric's color.

One of the thread types you could work with for your project includes decorative thread. It is slightly denser than the normal thread. You would also notice that the thread exists in different colors and varieties. It is quite different from the usual cotton and polyester sewing thread. It offers beauty to your project. For piecing and hand appliqué, you could easily work with the regular-weight cotton and polyester thread strings.

Another type of thread is metallic thread. This thread type helps to add a nice glow to your project. It is more delicate than the other threads used for decorations. They occur in two forms—the twisted metallic locks with piles twisted together like the traditional thread types. Then, there are the flat metallic threads that reflect as much light as possible. The only issue about them is that they are likely to melt when heat is applied to them.

After choosing out the top thread and a bobbin thread—with factors like the color and weight—get a bobbin fill to work along with. A bobbin fill is a fine thread that can easily be slotted into your bobbin. It can also be used in the manufacture of different kinds of thread.

When working on a project where the thread lines pop out, you could select a 40-weight thread for the top and a 50-weight thread for the bobbin. If you go for lighter weights of thread at the bobbin, you can reduce the number of times the bobbin thread is refilled.

| Thread size | Weight designation | Decorative thread type |
| --- | --- | --- |
| 20-weight | Very heavy | Metallic, polyester |
| 30-weight | Heavy | Polyester, rayon |
| 35-weight | Medium | Twisted rayon |
| 40-weight | Medium | Rayon, Polyester |
| 50-weight | fine | Cotton, Polyester |
| 60-weight | Very fine | Cotton, polyester |
| monofilaments | Extra-fine | Nylon, polyester |

**Needles**

Undertaking a quilting project with a fresh needle will help you save a lot of time and stress. Although universal needles work well for many quilters, some machines require a specialist needle. Pick up some size 80/12 topstitch needles when you're shopping for materials. These needles are longer, thinner, and stronger to assist you in getting through your fabric and batting layers. These needles are used by many quilters for all kinds of quilting, but they are especially useful for free-motion quilting.

**Batting**

A huge number of quilted projects require the use of batting. Batting is another layer of fabric that lies between the backing fabric and the ornate fabric at the top. The batting is usually of low-loft. Such batting types help refine the quilt art by giving it a steady or sturdy platform on which it sits.

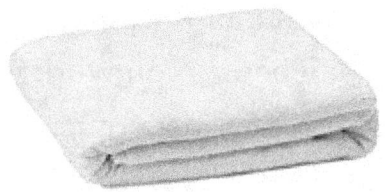

You should also ensure that you go for batting that has the following features;

- It should be easy to stitch
- It should be one that can last for a very long time, i.e., durability.
- It should be one that doesn't stretch so easily. That way, you can get your projects unruffled when they suspend down a hanger.
- It should be in the dimensions that are workable for your project.
- It should have a low bulk if you plan on washing your project very regularly.

In any case, if your batting comes out looking ruffled, you could try out any of the solution techniques listed out below;

- Take the batting out of the package and then have it unrolled a day before you work with it
- If appropriate to the fiber content, sprinkle water lightly across the surface. Then, have it tumbled within a dryer with an appropriate setting. Then, air-dry it.
- Buy a batting material of high quality.

**Marking Tools**

The more you quilt, the more plans you make. Now, as you make the most intricate quilting designs and projects, there would be a very high need for you to draw out marks that would stand in as reference points and boundaries. You could work with the usual water-soluble pencils when doing the marking, though. For continuous and fully lined stencils, you should get the full line stencils. Examples of the other marking tools include water-soluble pens and chalk.

## Pen and Paper

Practicing with a pen and paper before moving on to the actual art on your fabric would help you master the movement of your hands while minimizing the possibility of mistakes on the actual project. As you practice, the pen becomes the needle, and the paper becomes the fabric. The only difference is that the actual quilting requires you to move your quilt while the other requires you to move your pen.

You would notice at the end of the day that you'd end up moving your hands well enough in practice just the same way you would do for the actual quilting. For a practice to feel closer to the real project, you could switch the pen with a marker. More friction exists between the paper and the tip of the marker than between that of a pen. The presence of friction is another issue you'd face when quilting the actual project.

**Quilting Rulers**

Free-motion quilting can be achieved with different designs—loops, curves, straight lines, etc. When fused to your project, all of these effects or features would help add more focal centers. The quilting ruler plays more roles when you are quilting straight lines. If you quilt these lines, you would only get the best effect when using a ruler. There are different kinds of rulers for quilting are;

- Curved rulers
- Straight rulers
- Rulers for special designs like hearts, feathers, and circles.

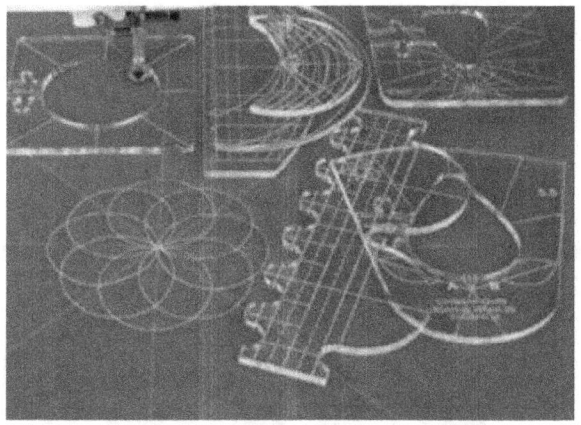

**Basting Pins**

The best basting pins to use for your free-motion quilling projects are curved basting pins. A pack that contains about fifty of them would probably be adequate if you are working on a small-scale quilting project.

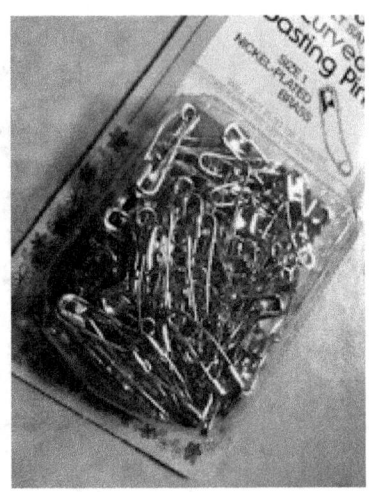

The other ways by which you could baste your projects are;

- With sprays
- With a basting gun.

**Scissors**

As you quilt, you would notice that you'd have to cut through strings of threads about a 'hundred' times. This is where your pair of scissors comes in. You want to ensure that they are close to you at all times as you work on your project. One tip you could work with is by hanging a pair of scissors down your neck. That way, you'd have them very close to you.

## Quilting Gloves

While quilting, it would be great for you to have extra gripping. This extra grip would help you rotate the fabric as you quilt your designs through it. The gloves you could go for are very lightweight and breathable. However, for perfect gripping, you should go for rubber gloves. Those kinds of gloves would provide a better gripping than the one you'd get from cotton gloves.

Although you can choose not to work with quilting gloves, however, the reasons below are why you should go for a pair of quilting gloves;

1. Working without gloves causes you to grip the fabric with more force which practically imposes more tension within the muscles of your upper hand. The tension would cause the muscles of your neck to become even tenser.
2. Secondly, the gloves and the friction it offers as you work on your project allow you to navigate the project easily. All you need to do is place your gloved fingers around the working needle in a

triangular form. When needed, you could easily adjust your hands.

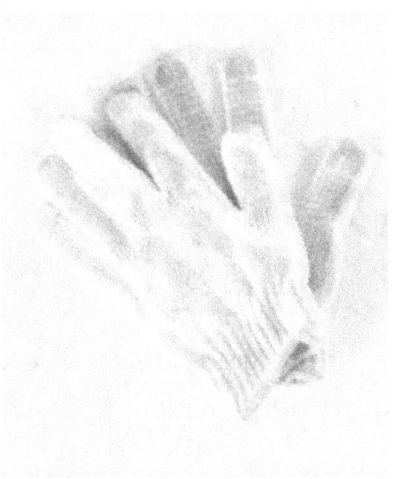

**Supreme Sliders**

The supreme sliders are sheets of Teflon that you place between the bed of your machine and the quilted project. They work to cancel out or minimize the effect of the friction that exists between the machine's surface and the worktable. It also ensures the free movement of the quilt.

With these sliders, you can also create even more beautiful designs with a reduced strain on the muscles of your body. One face of the slider is pink and filled with dots that aid your grip. The other side is sleek and fixed in a face-up direction. The hole at the middle should be aligned at all times with the hole that exists in your machine. This slider works to keep the feed dogs covered and prevent the quilt from having contact with them.

You need to know that the supreme sliders are wonderful tools that should be handled carefully because of how delicate they are. If you are using them for the first time, you could find it very easy to keep the corners taped down with masking tapes. At least, that could continue until you adjust to the way it feels beneath the quilt.

**Free-Motion Machine Foot**

This is one of the most important supplies you need in free-motion quilting. To quilt using the free-motion style, you have to have this foot. In some cases, it is referred to as the darning foot. Its function is to slide across the fabric to ensure that it remains in one place while the stitches are run through. So, if you are making styles that run in different directions, you can be sure that the machine foot would help keep the fabric down.

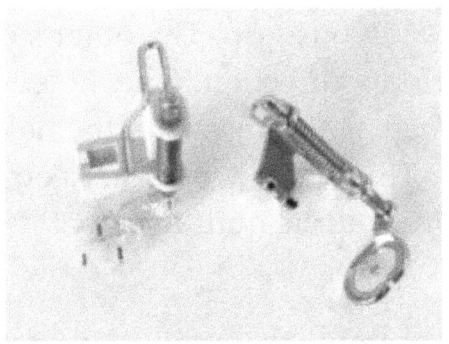

There are different types of this machine foot—some are made out of plastic, and the others are made out of metal. Some have open toes, and others have closed toes. Whatever you choose to work with boils down to the kind of style you'd prefer. In some cases, you'd find one that comes with your sewing machine.

When buying a machine foot, ensure to check if your machine is of the low or high shank. The word 'shank' refers to the distance between the end of the foot and the screw used to keep it fixed to the machine. The low shanks measure about ¾", and the high shanks measure about 1" or more. The very common sewing machines have shanks of the low category. But then, to be sure, you could measure the shank with a ruler or peruse the manual that comes with it.

**Setting Up Your Quilting Workarea**

The instructions below will get you started with setting up your workarea.

1. The sewing machine is the one machine you'd be working with the most. So, you want to make sure it is located in a place that provides you with the highest level of ease. You should also recall that you'd be fixing to your sewing machine an extra tabletop that will create more space for your project. So, yes, the sewing machine would take up most of the space. You also want to have another inch of space around the machine if you want to move around it as you work. Remember, it's Free-motion quilting. The sewing machine could be placed next to a window so that you remain cool as you work.
2. Next, ensure that you fix as many lights as possible to illuminate your workplace. The lighting issue becomes more important when the color of the thread you are working with blends with the fabric you are using. That way, you'd

end up straining your eyes way too much if you do not have a proper lighting system.
3. Get a chair that helps you sit a reasonable distance above ground level. The distance should be easily adjustable. This will help you ensure that you have a better view of the project you are making. The chair you go for should have all of these features combined;
    - Stability: A stable chair sits on about five legs. That way, when you shift or move, it doesn't fall over.
    - Adjustability: The chair you get should be one whose height above the ground can easily be adjustable. If you want to sit higher or lower, you'd want to be able to adjust your chair for that to happen. You also want to ensure that your knees are inclined through an angle of ninety to get things pretty comfortable for you. Also, you'd want a chair that keeps your feet firmly planted on the floor.

- Presence or absence of arms: For a better quilting experience, it is recommended that you get chairs without arms. Now, this choice depends entirely on you. Some quilters prefer chairs that have extra supports for their arms as they work. However, you should also know that these arms could prevent you from tucking your chairs under your table when you want to have a very close view of whatever you are doing.
- Presence or absence of wheels: The presence or absence doesn't matter. This too depends on whatever you like. They just make it easy for you to move about.
- Comfort: To ensure that you'd be comfortable sitting on the chair for long, you should ensure that you sit on it before you make a purchase.
4. After getting your chair, you'd need to decide how you want it placed within your workspace. You should ensure that you sit with your body

right in front of the needle. In all, you should also see to it that your hips, waist, and shoulders all lie in the same line. You shouldn't have to lean in or out. That way, you could also deal easily with eventual tiredness.

5. Next, you want to ensure that the quilt you are working on has all the support it needs for a perfect project. The technique of free-motion quilting mandates the quilt to move. You want to ensure that to the side lies a platform that would support the quilt. If you are also working on very large quilt projects, you might also want to add more platforms behind the sewing machine. An example of this extra support platform is an adjustable banquet table.

6. Make use of metallic stands for your cones and not plastic ones. Cones are items that help to keep your threads in place. Plastic cones have been noted to stir up static current, which the metallic ones wouldn't. The latter is more massive and stable than the former. Also, when using thread whose strings were wound together in a

crisscross fashion, the cones will help ensure that they do not get messy. Metallic stands also help to ensure that you can maximize your space the best way possible.
7. Your tools should be within your reach. You could keep a small unit or shelf right behind you as you quilt so that you can easily reach out to pick whatever tools you need as you work. You could also place your instruction manual close if you need to verify something.
8. Make your workspace inviting. You can create the right ambiance for your workspace by bringing in television, radio, or anything that would fill the air with nice tunes. You could also have scented candles burning around the room to give you the encouragement you need to start some work. Then, lastly, you could have a room where you display your quilted projects. All of the arrangements you make should propel you to get the best results at the end of the day.

**Getting Your Machine Up and Ready**

Before you can start any quilting project, you have to ensure that your sewing machine is up and ready for work. You also want to ensure that it is without dust or dirt before starting. For details on how to de-fluff your sewing machine, check the manual that came with it. Once you are done with the cleaning, continue with the procedures listed out below;

1. Fix the quilting foot (darning foot) to the machine. If these do not come with the machine, you can buy them separately. That is why you should seriously consider the features you need for your quilting project before going ahead to purchasing any sewing machine.
2. To fix the darning foot, which could be square or oval, screw the normal foot out of its place and replace it with the darning foot. If you are working with a foot with an open toe, you'd see your stitches form and thread the needle. That may not be possible when working with a closed toe. The steps below describe how you can have your darning foot fixed;

- Lower the feed dogs on your machine (the instruction on this comes with your manual)
- With a screwdriver, disengage the foot from the machine
- Align the darning foot in such a way that the long metallic end extends through the hooks on the needle rod. The needle rod is that part of the machine you unscrew when you want to get your needle out.
- Screw-in the darning foot to the claw-like grips.

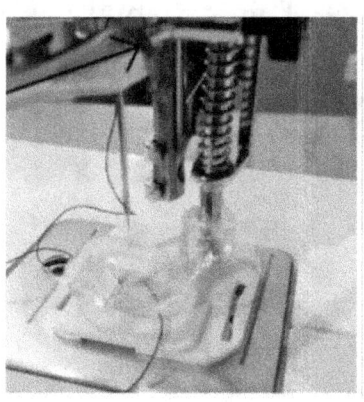 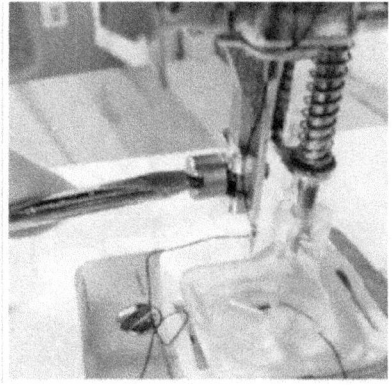

3. Next, drop the feed dogs. There's a control for this at the side or back of your machine. You can check the manual for the location if it is in neither place. If you forget to set your feed dogs back up after you finish your Free-motion quilting, your fabric will not go through the machine when you return to regular sewing. Upon fixing your feed dogs back up, adjust your balance wheel until your feed dogs come up through the stitch plate.
4. Set the length of the stitches to zero or to a lower length as you can.
5. Check to see if your needle is in an automatic down position. This is the button with two triangles on my machine. This capability is not available on all machines, but if it is, it is quite handy for Free-motion work.

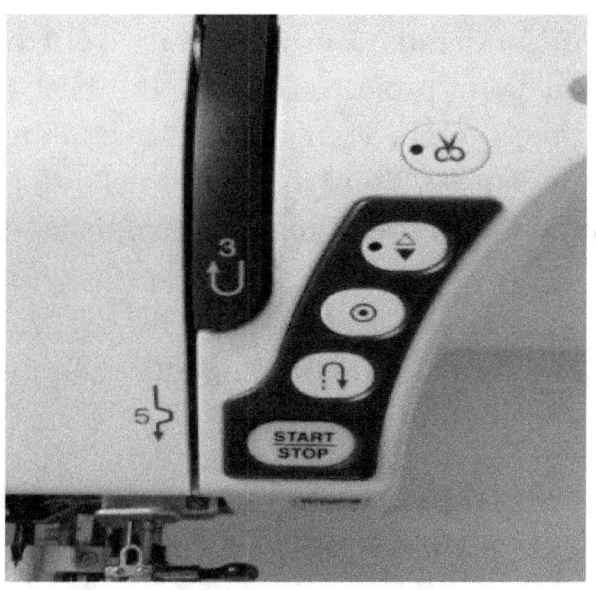

6. Now, you can alter the speed of the machine if you want. Some would rather prefer they work the machine at high speeds. The issue with that choice is that it doesn't allow you to exercise enough control as you quilt.
7. Your sewing machine is now fully set up and ready for quilting.

**Practicing Your Free-Motion Quilting On Paper**

One trick most quilters do not yet know is that any design that can be quilted can be drawn out on paper first. Practicing manually with a pen and paper will help you understand how to place your hands as you work on your project. To quilt the best projects, you would need to get your muscles acquainted with your hand movement. You would also need to get your eyes acquainted with following your hands as you draw out the pattern. To familiarize yourself with the art of drawing designs, it would be best if you just spent hours and more hours filling pages with different styles and patterns of quilting.

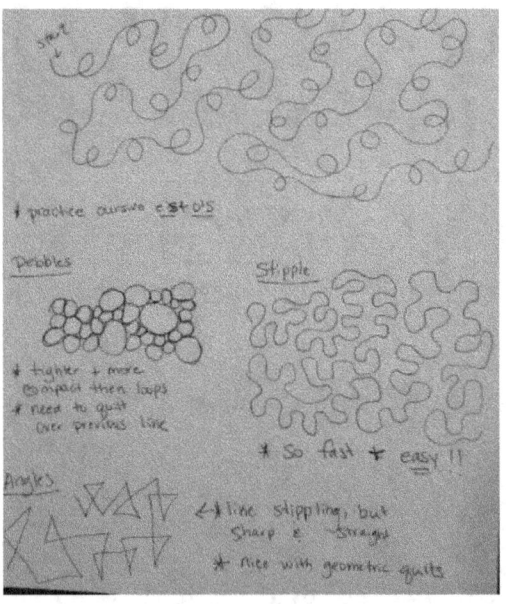

Now, after you must have used a sheet of paper and pen to test your quilting skills or to prepare yourself for the actual quilting, you can go ahead to try it out on your fabric. Squares of scrap fabric or unusable batting fabric would work best for testing out your quilting skills. That way, you'd be able to see or decipher how your project would look when done on the real fabric. All of these help to ensure you get better at quilting great designs. It also helps to reduce the amount of errors you make while working.

**Popular Designs In Free-Motion Quilting**

Free-motion quilting allows a lot of versatility and flexibility. It also enables you to be as creative as you desire. You could fuse it with the walking-foot quilting or the ruler-work quilting. You could make your free-motion design the main deal or the side deal. You could use the designs to fill up spaces or merge two separate areas. The list goes on and on. However, learning the basic techniques is vital as a beginner.

So, we will touch nine of the standard free-motion quilting designs that a beginner should know of before they begin to quilt;

**Loops**

This design technique is the first you'd need to learn as a quilter. When you make loops, you will notice that your arms travel in the 'L' direction. It would look more or less like you are drawing the shape out.

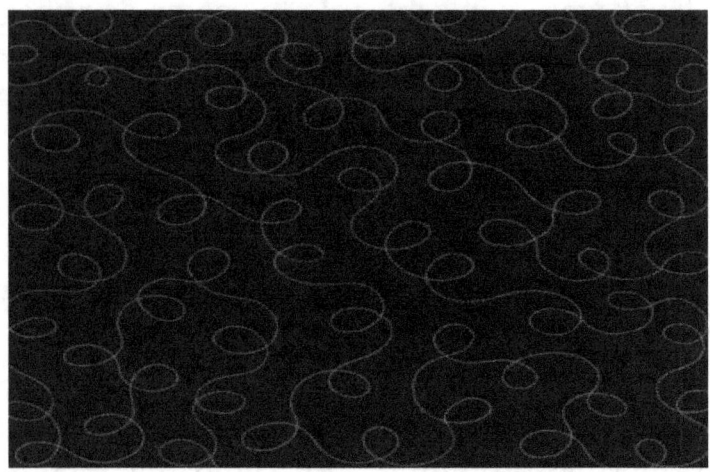

This style remains the same whether you are using the stand-up long arm or the sit-down domestic sewing machine. These loops usually occur in different sizes. When it is made small, you'd mostly use it in filling up blank spots in a quilted project. However, when it is made large, it stands in for filling up spaces with bigger dimensions.

**Getting started with loops**

The first loops that we will access are the meandering loops, which are user-friendly. They are mostly used in filling up squares of empty spaces on a project. The thing about the loops here, though, is that they are all connected, so, when quilting, you feel more like you are writing something out cursively.

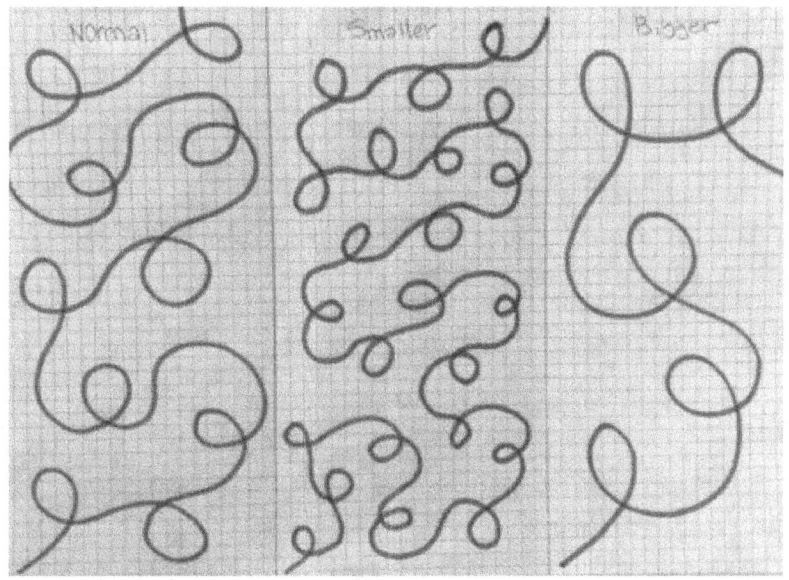

We will practice with pen and paper until we get used to the curves as with all free-motion quilting designs. As you draw out these loops, you might want to put the following tips at the back of your mind;

- The project comes out nicer when the loops have different shapes. You don't need to get perfectly round circles.

- You could try to plant some space between your loops and then see if you'd like the look on your project.
- Avoid fixing rows between the loops.
- If you are going to use these loops to fill squares of empty space, ensure that you don't have many loops in a row. Just make about two loops in each and every direction possible—not in the same plane.
- Your batting allows for the stitches to have relevant spacing between them.

Once you are done practicing, you can then move on to the actual quilting.

- First, you might want to practice on a scrap piece of fabric. Cut out a square of the fabric of 14" and then other squares for the batting and backing.
- Move to your machine, and set the speed to medium (this option is for those working with the electrically-pedaled machines)
- Start from the bottom and work your way up the block with the meandering loops.

- As you quilt, try to move around to different locations so that you don't fill up rows of fabric with similar loops

**Pebbles, Bubbles, Pearls**

Pebbles, sometimes known as bubbles, pearls, or circles, are a natural extension of loops. You're forming the same shape as before, but this time it's closer together. Because they're so close together, your eye will pick up on any inconsistencies fast, so don't strive to make them all the same size. The best bet is to go with natural variations. With pebbles, you'll end up stitching over a region several times, resulting in a thread build-up. And the more densely you quilt, the stiffer your quilt and the more thread you will see.

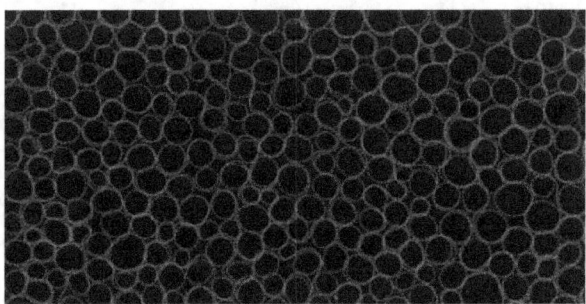

The picture below shows a perfect representation of these shapes.

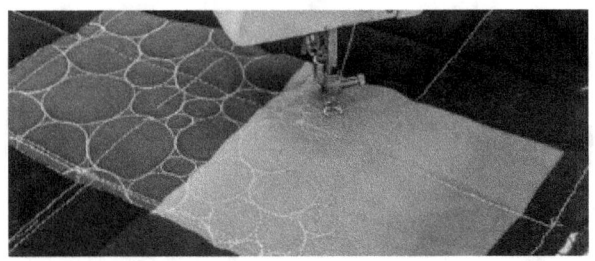

Making pebbles usually require that you stitch one line over another line. The issue with this style of quilting is the time it takes to make. So, you might want to reconsider having to make this design all over the surface of your quilt.

Pebbles are best used in conjunction with other quilting designs and not as the main design element. For example, it would be great to use this design to make the borders of your quilted project by filling the single square only and not the whole quilt. The two techniques you could work with when making these pebbles;

- **Filled Pebbling**: Filled pebbling is an excellent choice for the best effect and intensity since it amps up the travel stitching and thread play to make the design pop out much more on your quilt.

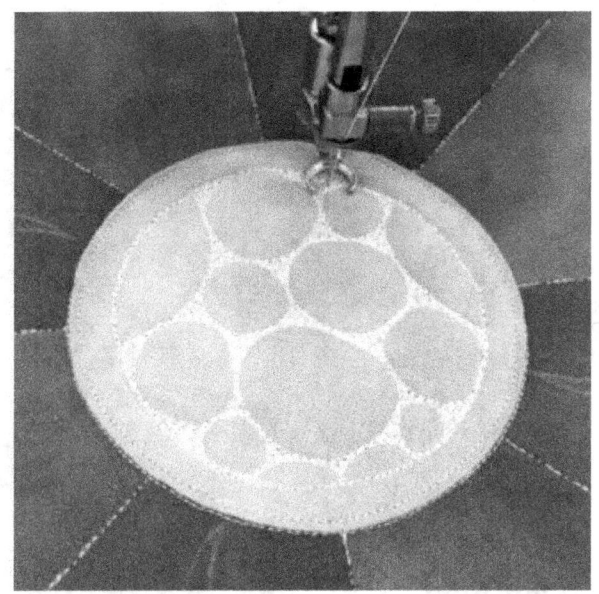

- **Underwater Rocks**: This style of making pebbles is one that you should go for when you have an issue making smooth and regular circles. The design utilized here ends up looking quite messy, and that is usually the way it is. It helps you to gain mastery in making circular movement of pebbles easily.

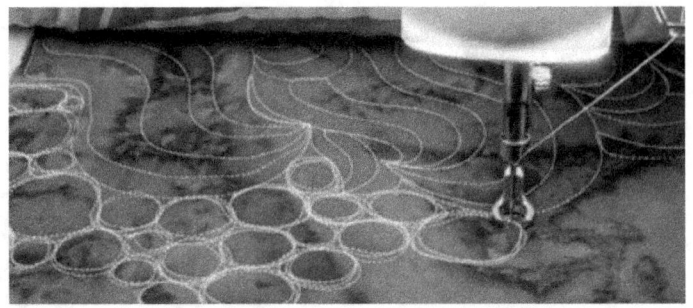

**Tips when quilting pebbles on a domestic machine**

- Quilting small pebbles on a domestic machine are actually easier. The smaller the circular forms, the less movement your hands make, and the more likely you will move the quilt smoothly and avoid ending up with a strange amoeba form rather than a circle.
- Large pebbles could be quite difficult to quilt out on large squares of fabric when working with domestic sewing machines. This is because you would have to turn the quilt around to get the perfect circle. That 'turning around' reduces the weight and the size of the quilt you come out with finally. It also limits how much you can spread your hands apart as you work.

- You also would not be able to adjust the quilt without the circles having one or more wagging curves. Once you notice the wag, reduce the size of the pebble. That way, you can quilt the circles in one move instead of you having to stop midway for adjustment.

**Tips when quilting pebbles on a long arm machine**

- With a long arm machine, you can make circles or pebbles in any dimension you desire. You could also finish a pebble in a shorter time. However, the issue here is that the stitch lines may not be too clean as it could be hard to establish a proper level of coordination.

  Also, when you turn your machine around for the pebbles, you'd find out that the force of inertia tends to push the needle out of line. So, most times, you have to hold on to it tight and firm not to lose control.

  What you can do to solve this issue is reduce the force that you apply to the machine's handles. That way, the long arm machine would end up moving easily. You also need to remember that the beauty in free-motion quilling only comes out when you can move your hands as easily as possible.

- To have a good level of control as you quilt pebbles, starting with underwater rocks, could go a long way in helping you manage the speed you work with. You also get to form better circles.

**Meander and Stipple**

This design is the go-to filler in Free-motion quilting. A meander rarely runs over itself; instead, it squirms in and out of the way in an evenly spaced manner. You'll. A stipple is similar to a meander, but it's a little tighter and excellent for filling smaller areas.

**What to know when meandering or stippling**

Several basic stitching rules apply to free-motion filler designs. These rules are as straightforward to remember as the rules for cursive writing. You'll be capable of quilting anywhere once you know the design rules and practice quilting it.

- Stippling follows a fairly basic rule: stitch a wavy, meandering line that does not cross itself. It's vital to remember that this rule only applies to stippling. Many new quilters have been misled into believing they are not to cross their quilting lines at all. Please note that crossing your quilting lines is totally acceptable, and many quilting designs involve crossing and travel stitching to make the design.
- Drawing stippling on paper is a fantastic technique to practice because the same mental muscles used to sketch the design will be utilized to quilt it.

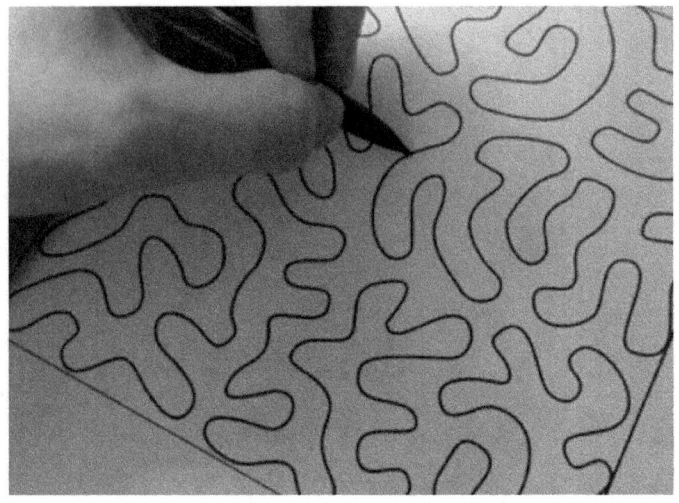

- Stippling has a distinct texture that looks to flatten or fade into a quilt's background. It's ideal for densely quilting into the background portions of a whole-cloth quilt or quilting a soft bed quilt on a wide scale.
- Stippling is an excellent quilting design to master since it teaches you how to move the quilt smoothly, estimate space, echo the quilt, and manage it. Stippling is also quite adaptable, as it can be used on any quilting scale and may be quilted across vast areas quickly.

## Paisley

This is a lovely design that gives your quilt a sleek and elegant touch. For better imagery, paisley is more like half the outline of a complete heart or a feather. The outline for paisley usually goes from wide to narrow, and most times, you'd have to pair it with geometric quilting. The style of geometric quilting will be discussed in the next quilting style. The paisley design is great for beginners.

### Quilting paisley the free-motion way

- The basics for quilting paisley are straightforward: start by stitching a teardrop shape. Pivot the shape and quilt an echo around it. Increase the gap between the lines as you stitch around the curve, then pull them nearer together while you return to the beginning position.
- You can pivot an echo as many times as you want around the teardrop shape before branching out and stitching another shape in a new direction. Stitch additional teardrop shapes with echoes pouring over your quilt to expand the design.

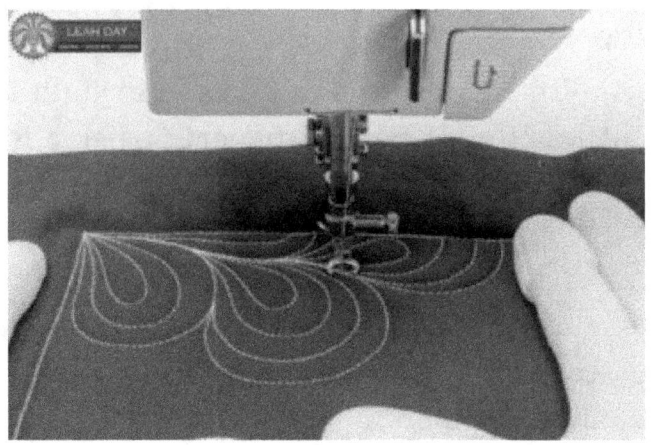

**Pro-Tip**

The travel stitching and additional thread that develops around the beginning point of the individual teardrop shape is what makes paisley very tricky. When I began quilting for the first time, this is where I encountered problems. My thread would break every time I reached another stitching line. At the time, I was Free-motion quilting using cotton thread that was very coarse and weak. For the same reason, I battled in quilting pebbling, and while I adored both designs, I couldn't bear my thread breaking each time a single shape was stitched.

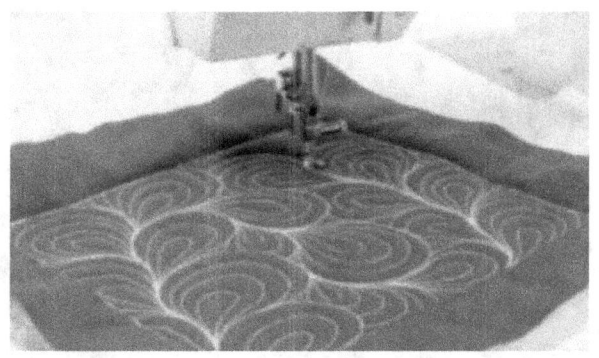

Then I found the Isacord thread, which allowed me to stitch paisley, pebbling, and any other design I desired. Isacord is a 40-weight polyester embroidery thread that is both thin and sturdy, allowing you to travel stitch over the same area numerous times.

**Teardrops**

Because it fills space while establishing a trail back, the example below uses doubled or even tripled teardrops, which some quilters consider simpler. You will also realize we didn't always meet back where we started, as some of the teardrops are "open." That's absolutely OK! This is a versatile and attractive shape. Variating your teardrops size, like with any Free-motion shapes, is fine since you are less likely to see abnormalities. It also adds a more personal touch to it.

To start practicing this design, begin at the top left corner, create a short clockwise loop around it, then swap directions, making a counterclockwise loop around it. Then do it again. You can begin a fresh "teardrop" at any time but note that the loops don't move back to the start of that specific loops; instead, they "bounce" off previous loops.

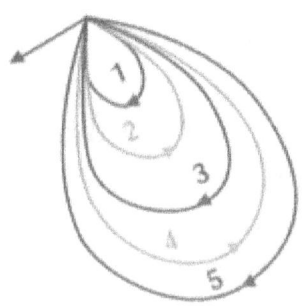

## Feathers

Feathers have a classic, elegant appeal that works well with many traditional quilts—and even those that aren't so traditional! They can be freeform curved around the quilt or formed into wreaths or vines. Feathering is regarded as intermediate or advanced since it needs a certain amount of comfort and confidence when free-motioning. (Mastering teardrops is a good place to start because the movement is comparable.) Depending on your level of comfort or desired look, feathers might come from a sewn spine or not. You can start small and work your way up, or you can be more haphazard. You can also examine the work of other quilters and try new things to establish your own style.

## Swirls

Swirls are a natural progression from teardrops. It takes a little practice because they don't cross over and normally have consistent spacing between stitching. It'll be well worth it! Swirls have a childlike touch to them that may add a lot of fun and delight to a quilt. And, like many of these free-motion fillers, it may be scaled down to fill smaller spaces or customized to fill larger spaces.

Let's take a look at some other 'designs' quickly

**Geometric**

Straight-line, geometric quilting is probably one of the more difficult Free-motion designs to master. Being able to free-hand a straight design is a crucial skill, especially when you are unable to grab a ruler or switch to a walking foot. Abnormalities such as 45-degree angles and parallel lines will pop up instantly to your eyes. On the other hand, the geometric shapes have a distinct appearance and feel.

**Vining Leaves**

Creating vines that produce leaves instead of loops is a fun and practical variant of loops. For some, the leaf shape comes effortlessly, while it takes some skill for others. It can be made with or without a vein, a sharp or rounded tip, a large or tiny size, and it always provides a fresh, natural aesthetic that fits well with a variety of designs.

**Vining Flowers**

Add vining flowers to take it to the next level! The loop has been turned into a flower. Flowers, while more difficult, can be made more forgiving with a few strategies. First, don't take your time getting to the center of the circle. When you overthink a circle, you're more likely to get an ellipse. Second, ensure the petals aren't all the same size but rather have a natural variety of similar sizes. Finally, add a few basil leaves to take a break from the strenuous motion of the flowers, and it will also look beautiful as part of the design.

Mastering a few free-motion fillers, whether working on a domestic or longarm sewing machine, will go a long way to help you in your free-motion quilting journey. To practice the motion of the designs, create a "sampler" as we did in previous steps. Some will come naturally, while others will take some time to master. Choose which ones you wish to improve and concentrate on them. You'll find yourself returning to that sampler and selecting different Free-motion designs to attempt as you become familiar with the machine, the movement, and the options available for batting and thread.

## Chapter 5

## Free-Motion Quilting Projects

Now that you know all there is to learn about free-motion quilting, we'd move right into the practice of quilting some of the designs into actual quilting projects.

**Note:** You can use more than one free-motion quilting design on your project, as I have done in the case below, and you can be creative with your own designs and do what works for you as I did in some of the projects in this chapter.

Also, keep in mind that having prior knowledge of quilting will be very helpful, so you don't get thrown off by some methods and terms mentioned in the projects.

### Quilted Placemats

This placemat is great for adorning your dining room or some other place in your house. You could place a vase over it too, and lots more you can do with the placemats. This project requires you to run several practices with pen and paper before quilting. However, this tutorial will take you from sketching designs using pencil and paper into quilting four distinct placemats that will help you improve your free-motion quilting skills.

**Tools and Materials**

- ½ yard of main fabric
- 1/3 yard of four different fabric sides
- 1 ½ yard of backing and binding fabric
- 1 yard of batting
- Sewing machine
- Patchwork foot of grade number 97D
- Edgestitch foot of grade number 10D
- A free-motion presser foot or a stitch regulator
- A straight stitch throat plate
- A Microtex needle for piecing of grade number 70
- Jeans needle of grade number 90
- Cotton thread
- Basting spray

**Instructions**

1. Begin by cutting out the dimensions of fabric for the placemat.
    - For the main fabric, cut four pieces/ strips measuring 12 ½" by 8 ½"
    - For the fours sides of the side fabric, cut sixteen pieces/ strips measuring 3 ½" by 10 ½" dimensions
    - For the batting fabric, cut four pieces/ strips measuring 20" by 14"
    - For the backing fabric, cut four pieces/ strips measuring 20" by 14"

2. Use the straight stitch plate, patchwork foot, and needle to set up the machine. The cotton thread should be used to thread the machine.
3. Sew four of the 3 ½" pieces together to make a 12 ½" x 10 ½" placemat on one side. Repeat with the remaining pieces, tweaking the fabric sequence to create some flair. At the end of the individual pieced pieces, seam a 12 ½" x 8 ½" piece of the main fabric.

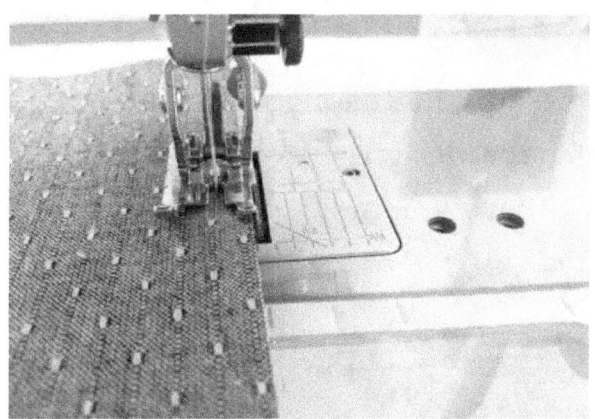

4. Place the batting on top of the backing. On top of that, set the pieced placemat. Baste the layers by spraying.
5. Attach the edgestitch foot to the needle, which should be in the middle position. Set the guide in

the seam's ditch and quilt-in-the-ditch placemat's five seams. Set the stitch length that you like.

6. Before quilting the placemats, you might want to sketch the designs beforehand to get a sense of how they will move before replicating on the fabric.

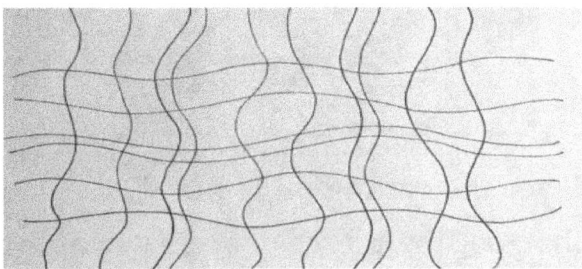

7. On the end of the fabric, start by quilting smooth wavy lines up and down. From one end of the

fabric to the other, stitching will be made. The lines might or might not repeat each other. To keep things interesting, adjust the spacing.

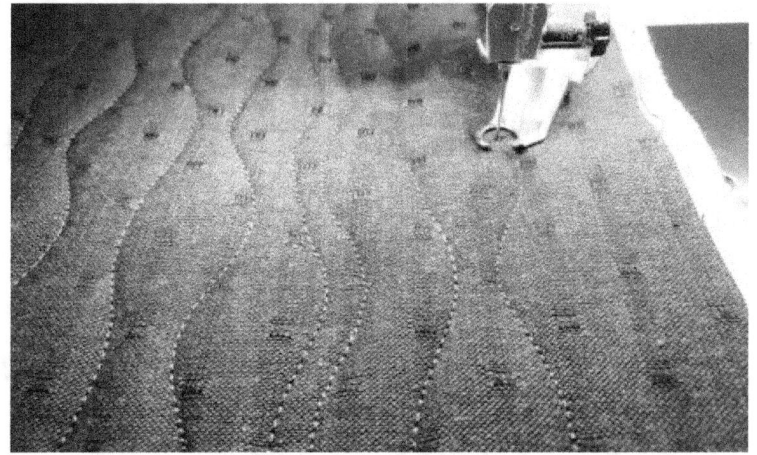

8. Sew the same wavy lines horizontally once the vertical lines have been sewn. Fill the fabric's whole piece. There's no need breaking the thread at the sewing line's end; simply continue stitching to the next row since the stitching will be hidden in the seam.

9. Place the fabric so that the quilted end is facing away from you and the four strips are nearest to you. Mentally count the strips from left to right

(1-4) while you look at them. The individual strip will be quilted in a unique way.

10. Strip 2 is the first to be worked on. Now that you've mastered the movements; up and down, left and right, let's merge the movements to stipple the strip. Make a pattern as shown below.

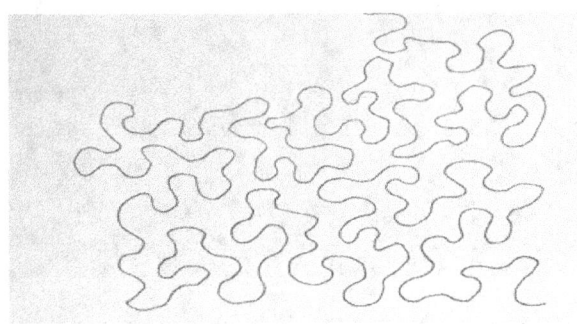

11. Pull up the bobbin thread in the seam that connects the strips to the quilted fabric. Fasten the thread, then stipple the strip from the raw edge in a gentle manner.

12. Go to the first strip. This second design follows the same rounded movement like the stipple, but with the added benefit of forming a point. This appears to be a step up from the basic stipple, and I refer to it as "stippling with attitude." On paper, practice the movement until you feel comfortable.

13. Begin stitching in the seam's ditch and continue across and below the strip, echoing where necessary.

14. Proceed to Strip 3, where we'll quilt pebbles to refine our circular movement. Pebbles don't need to be completely round or uniform in size. In a clockwise manner, draw a circle. Proceed around the circle, then draw a second circle in a counterclockwise manner.

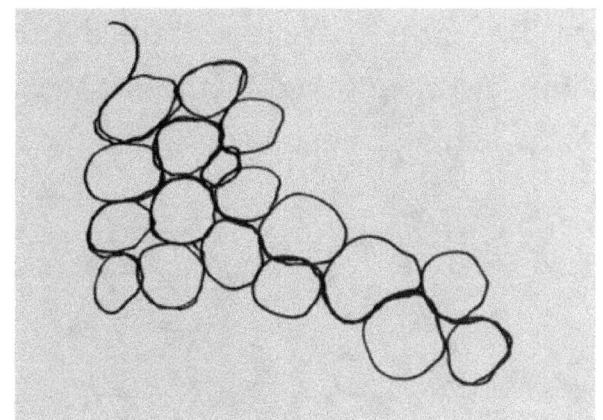

15. Each circle should be started in the opposite direction as the preceding one. And travel wherever you want by using the edges of the circles. Use the pebble design to fill strip 3, constantly traveling on the pebble's outside edge.

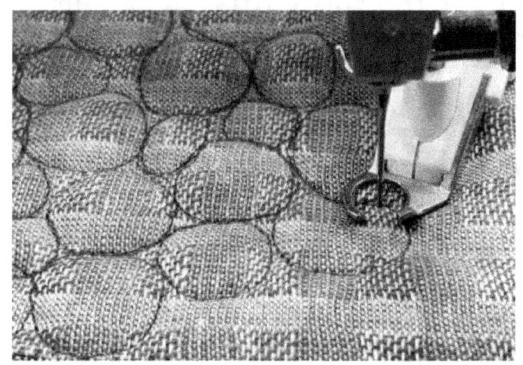

16. Proceed to strip 4. We'll practice the three prior designs by integrating them into one. Redraw them, switching from one design to the next.

17. When you're ready, move on to the strip and stitch the design combinations
18. Repeat for the individual placemat, changing the arrangement of the designs in the strips to enhance the look in the set of placemats.
19. Placemats should be squared and bound.

**Quilted Potholder**

Anyone can make this easy quilted potholder, whether you're changing worn-out hot pads, improving your sewing or quilting abilities, or seeking a customized gift. This project is gratifying and helpful, and it only requires a few supplies.

**Tools and Materials**

- Sewing machine
- ¼ yard of two individual coordinating fabrics (for the front and the back) or two fat quarters.

- For the binding— 1/6 yard of coordinating fabric
- ¼ yard of Insul-Bright fabric (a thin batting-like fabric with one side having an insulating material and the batting on the other side)
- Two pieces of 9" by 9" cotton fabric for the batting
- Coordinating thread.

**Instructions**

1. Cut two 8.5" square pieces of fabric, one for the top and the other for the bottom. Bigger sizes can be made by increasing the measurements by 1/2"

2. Cut out a piece of Insul-Bright and a piece of batting, both measuring 9" (both should be ½" bigger than the cutouts of the fabric). If you're going up a size, add ½" to the measurement.

3. Cut the strips for the binding. If creating a bigger potholder, cut the fabric into 2.5" x WOF (width of fabric) strips. If you are working with a smaller fabric piece, you'll need a total length of around 40". Because this potholder's fabric is small and the intention was to quilt two potholders (hopefully), many strips were cut.

4. For the binding, sew the strips together to make a long strip. Place the right sides together, sewing with a ¼" seam to join.

5. With your fingers, press the ¼" seams open to reduce the density of the edges.

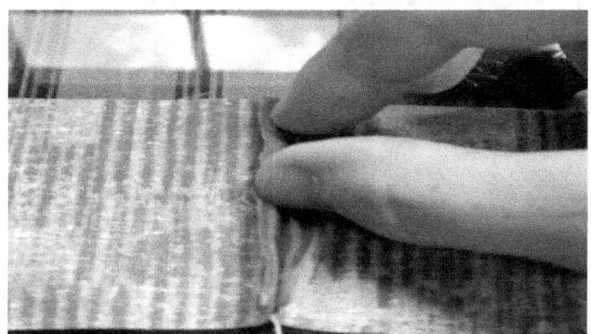

6. Press the strips in half.

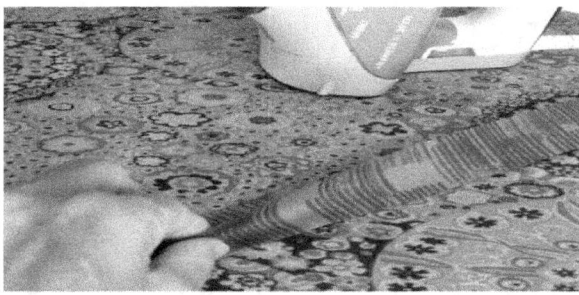

7. Press the strips you folded to make the final strips for binding

8. Place the fabric's bottom face down, cover it with the Insul-Bright and batting fabric, then overlay it with the top fabric face side up. Ensure the bottom and top fabrics are in line. You've just made a quilters "sandwich". Overhang the top and bottom pieces of fabric with the Insul-Brite and batting fabric.

Prepare your "sandwich" for quilting by pinning all the layers in 4-6 separate places along the edging.

9. All layers should be quilted together. To put it another way, sew the layers together. Then, use your sewing machine to quilt the meander style. You should use a thread whose color pops, unlike the one I used here

10. Trim the Insul-Bright and batting from the edges once you complete the quilting. The square's size will be around 8 ½". There's no need to be worried if your measurements fall slightly short.

Quilting can make the circumference "shrink" slightly.

11. Lay the finished binding strip from the previous step on the potholder's top side with the strip's raw edge (the side that's open) lined up with the hot pad's edge (the side that's folded and faces the potholder's center). Make a free allowance of binding (leaving a tail) of about 4 -5", then start to attach the binding using a seam allowance of ¼". Sew from the center of the pad and backstitch to fasten the end.

The objective of the "tail" and starting halfway along the length is to provide an opening after stitching ¾ of the way across the pad, providing space to attach the binding ends to complete it.

12. Sew the first side's edge by 1/4"—Backstitch to fasten and cut the threads. The image below provides a better description.

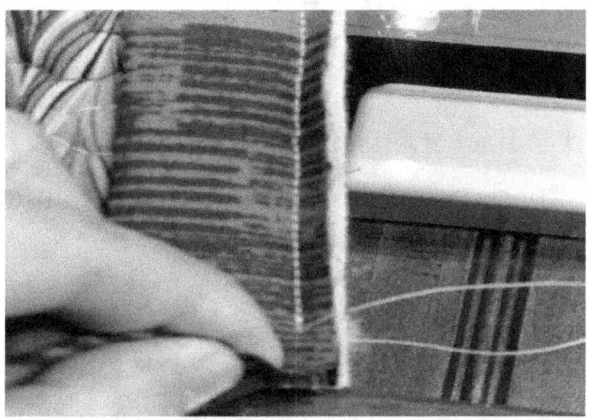

13. Remove the pad so you can readjust the binding strip and get it ready to attach it to the next side. Fold the binding strip to the right, perpendicular to where you previously sewed, with the raw edge aligned with the hot pad's next side edge

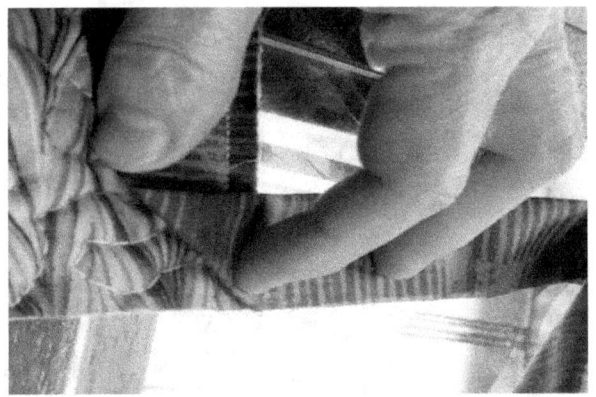

14. Fold it back to itself so that the strip's raw edges are lined up with the potholder's outside edge, making sure that the folded edge of the strip also lines up properly with the pad's top.

15. Start to stitch at the top and work your way down the side's length, backstitching to fasten

your stitches. Backstitch 1/4" from the edge, then cut the threads.

16. Repeat the instructions above to attach the binding across the hot pad. Stitch about 1/2" after turning the last corner, then backstitch to fasten.

17. After sewing the surrounding of the last corner and pausing around 1/2" in, there should be a 4-5" gap between the two binding ends on the last side.

18. Before going any further, the binding ends must be attached. Place the binding along the edges and locate their meeting point. Pinch them together to see where they join.

19. Open up the two binding pieces, placing their right sides side by side. The two binding pieces should be marked at their meeting point to make a stitch line.

20. Join the two binding pieces with a stitch (ensuring the right sides are lined up).

21. Trim the binding ¼" over the stitch line and open the seam with your fingers.

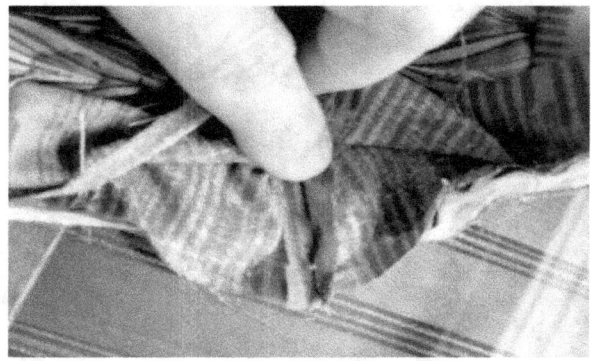

22. Lay down the binding again, this time with the raw edges toward the pad's edge, and finish the binding's attachment to the pad by backstitching to fasten it.

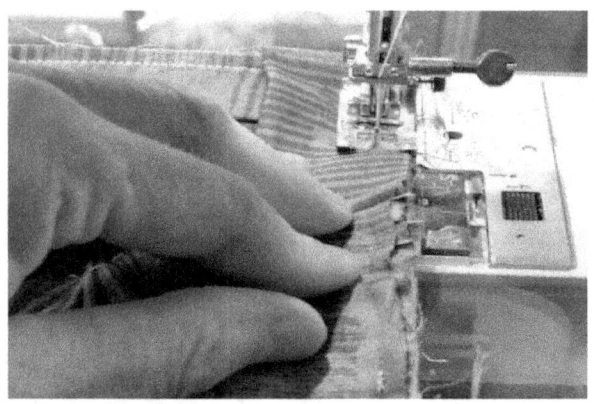

23. Turn the binding right side out, folding it across the hot pad's raw edge to cover the stitching on the other side, securing it with pins every 3-4".

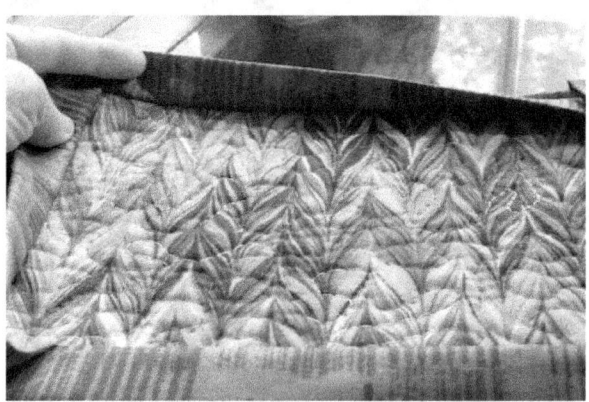

24. Hold down the binding's edge at the ¼" seam allowance area to make the corners.

25. Fold-down the next binding length and use a pin to secure it in place.

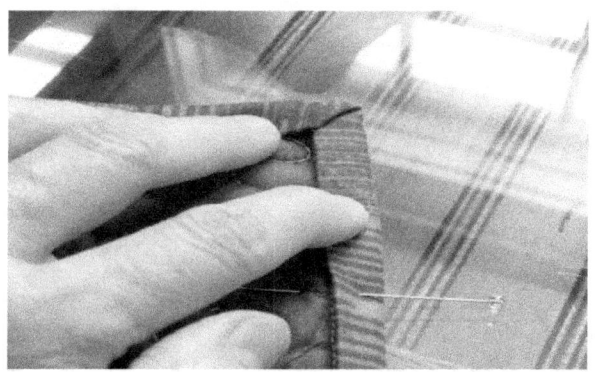

26. Repeat this process all the way across the potholder until all of the bindings are positioned to be stitched and secured. There are two ways to attach the leftover binding edge to the pad—sewing by machine (ditch stitching) or

by hand. Hand sewing is by far the neatest and easiest method, but it is also the most time-consuming.

27. With the front side up and starting in the center of one side of the hot pad, line the sewing needle with the "ditch" (where you attached the binding to the pad). Sewing in the ditch captures the binding's folded edge on the other side. Stitch all around and fasten with a backstitch.

28. You are done!

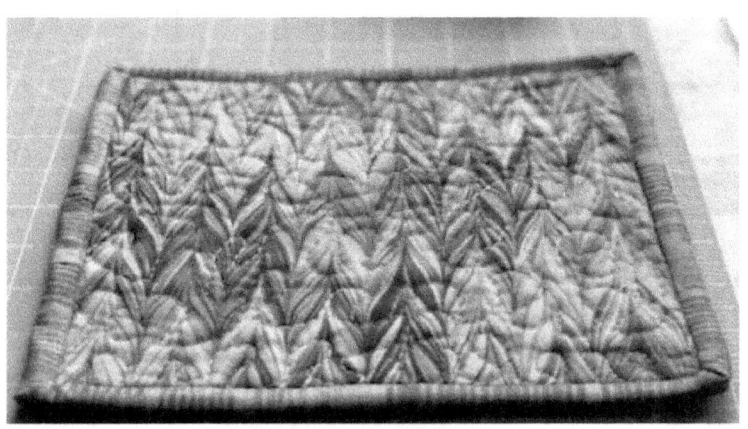

**Quilted Coasters**

These coasters have the appearance of a miniature quilt thanks to the pieced pieces of bright cotton and wavy, free-motion stitching. They make a great last-minute present for the holidays or any other special event.

Each coaster has an edgestitched frame that serves as the pivot point for the vertical wavy lines. The free-motion stitching turns up around the edgestitching but does not cross it. The wavy lines are not separate but instead a continual seam that travels up and down across the coaster. The best part is that there is no such thing as a bad move because it is entirely up to you. Allow your lines to intersect or even cross one another. The only advice I have is to stay within the frame of the edgestitching.

**Tools and Materials**

- A sewing machine
- A standard presser foot
- A seam foot of a quarter-inch (not too compulsory given all seams are ¼ inch)
- The edge guide foot (optional, but it would help keep the seam straight around the edge)

- Choose scraps or 1/4 yard cuts of 5 distinct fabrics for each coaster.

  **Note**: 10 matching fabrics from the Color Brigade collection were used to make the sets of four coasters in this design. We created two sets of matching fronts, but each of the four backs was unique.
- ¼ scrap yard of low loft batting
- A general-purpose thread that blends with the fabric
- A general-purpose slightly contrasting thread color for the free-motion quilting (tan was used here)
- Transparent ruler
- Iron and Ironing board
- A pair of scissors or a rotary cutting tool
- A cutting mat
- A seam gauge
- A seam ripping tool
- Straight pins

## Getting Started

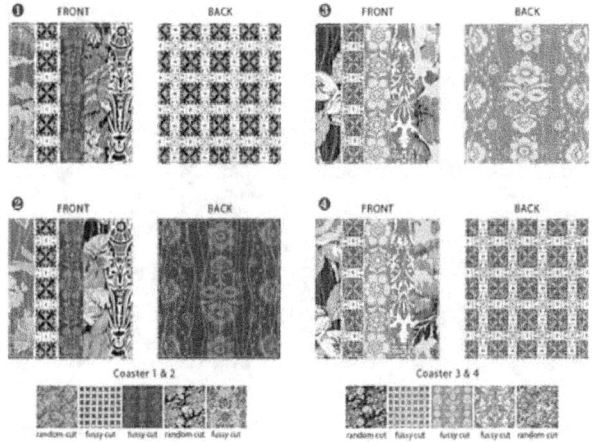

1. For EACH coaster, from the fabric, cut FIVE different 1½" wide x 5½" high strips plus ONE 5½" x 5½" square.
   NOTE: *As shown in our drawings above, some of our cuts were random and some were precisely fussy cut. When determining your cuts, remember to account for the ¼" seams.*
2. From the batting, cut ONE 5½" x 5½" square for each coaster.

## Instructions

### Prepare the patchwork for the front at the ironing board and sewing machine

1. Collect all 5 pieces of fabric making up the patchwork panel on the front. Arrange them in the correct sequence. The 5 pieces are stacked on

top of their corresponding backing square in the photo below.

2. Working from right to left, pin the first two pieces right sides together with one 5 ½ inch edge

3. Sew the two pieces together with a 1/4-inch seam allowance. We've raised the corner to reveal the two pieces being sewed.

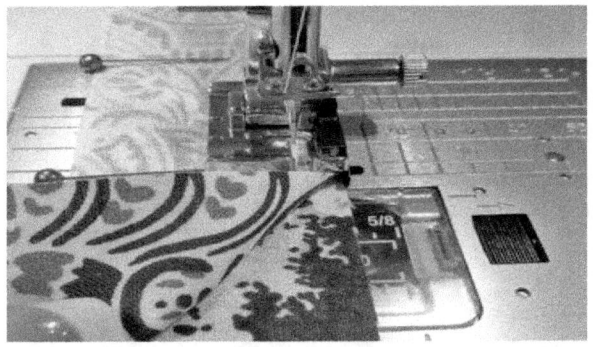

4. Stitch up the five pieces or strips by continuing with the same procedure discussed above.

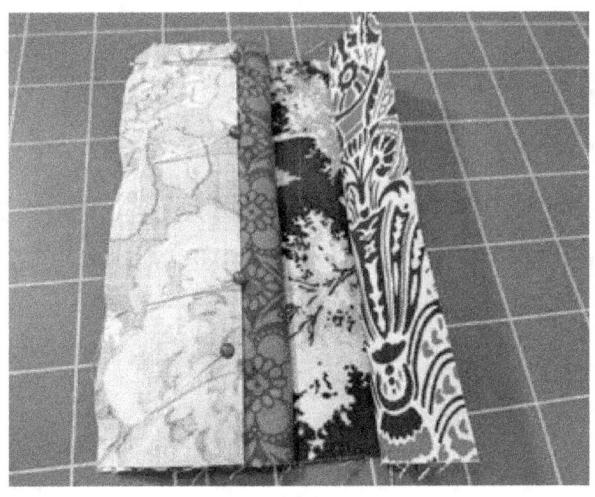

5. When you are done with the front panel, use an iron to press the ends flat. The seam allowances should be ironed towards the fabric with a darker hue.

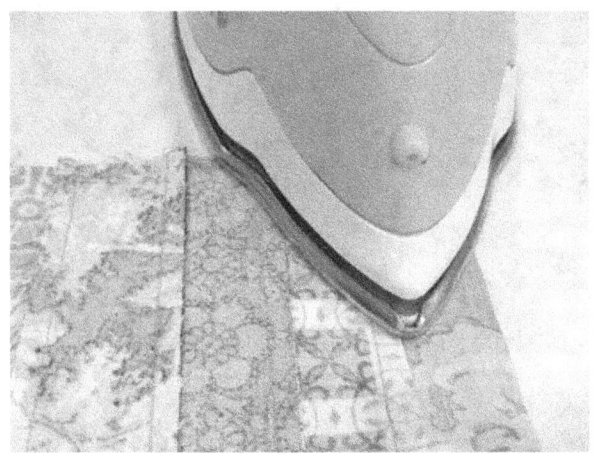

**Layering and stitching together**

6. Locate the batting square, then lay it on your work surface.
7. Find the square that will serve as the backing. Place it on top of the batting, right side up. Both layers should be flat on all four sides.

8. Place the patchworked front panel on the backing, right side down. Pin the 3 layers and make allowance for a 3 inch opening at the bottom.

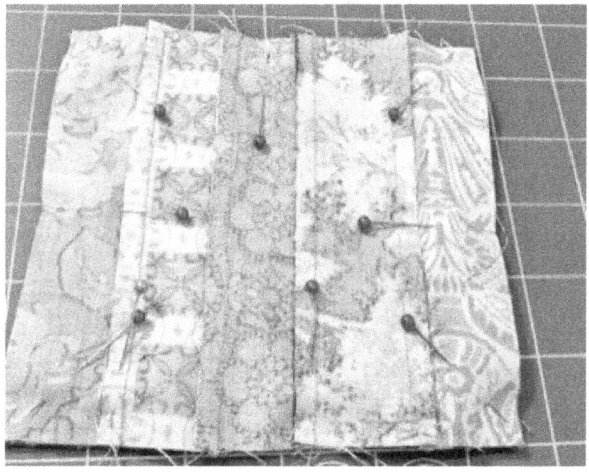

9. Run stitch lines around the four edges, while making sure to leave a seam allowance of about ¼."

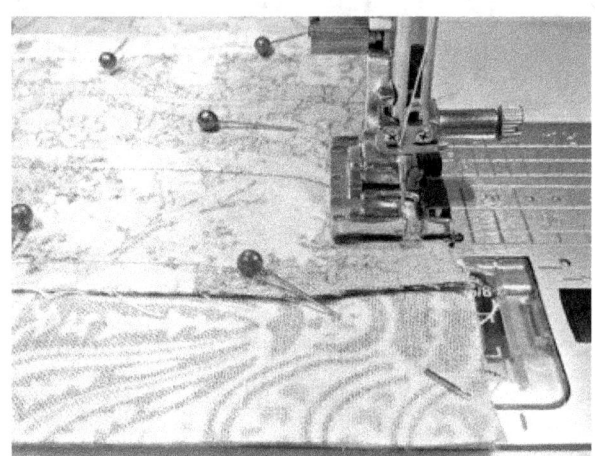

10. Keep in mind that each corner should be pivoted. And don't forget to close up your seam at the 3 inch opening of either side

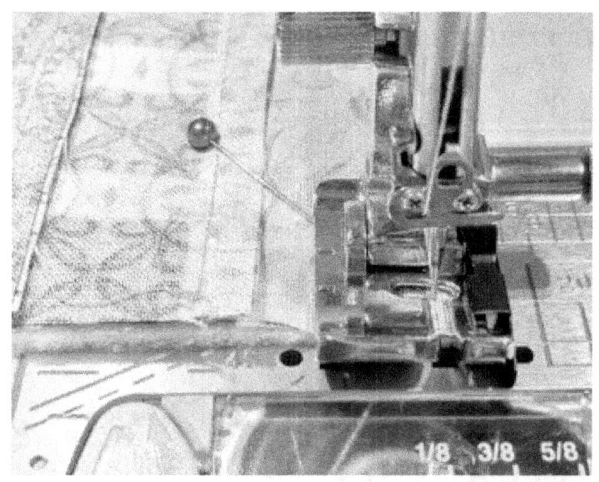

11. Press the seam allowance open with an iron before going ahead to cut off the corners diagonally with a pair of scissors.

### Turn, iron, **edgestitch**, and quilt

12. Via the opening, flip the coaster right side out. Carefully push the corners out with a knitting needle, chopstick, or a point turner to make them as sharp as they can be.

13. Press out the ends of the opening to lay flat alongside the seams.

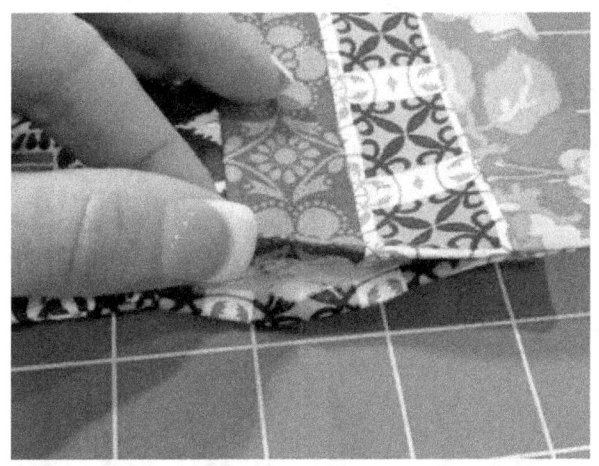

14. Replace the thread in your sewing machine with the slightly contrasting thread earlier mentioned (in this case, tan was used) and increase the length of the stitches.
15. Close up the opening with pins.

16. Edgestitch around the coaster's perimeter and pivot the individual corner. Janome Edge Guide foot was used to remain as near to the edge as possible while still achieving a nice and even stitch all the way around. The opening for turning is closed by this seam.

17. This is where we free-motion quilt the wavy lines. Note that you can be spontaneous and creative in your design choice like I did here (nothing is cast in stone). Remember, you need to insert a free-motion foot and drop the feed dogs on your machine to gain control over the movement of the fabric under the needle.

18. Ensure the lines of your waves are vertical while you follow the patchworked strips seams. Start at the corner ends of the edgestitching frame – about 1/8-inches from each corner then, move to the top of the frame.

19. Use the edgestitching as your pivot point when you arrive at it, then turn around and stitch in the reverse direction. Maintain a constant seam as you progress around the coaster.

20. The lines that snake your project should no doubt be wavy. Here you have the freedom to ensure that intersections occur between the lines. You could even allow the lines to bend a little bit off their normal path.

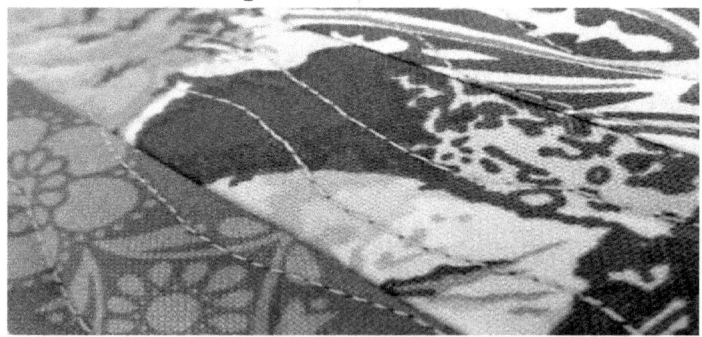

21. You are done with your project.

## Quilted Table Runner

Blocks and strips will be used to designate certain quilting locations in this strip-pie table runner. After that, I'll walk you through four basic quilting fills.

## Tools and Materials

- By Hand strip-pies by Benartex or a set of precut strips of 2 ½"
- Backing fabric of ½ yard
- Batting fabric of ½ yard
- Sewing machine (a long arm machine was used, but a domestic machine can also be used)
- Straight stitch needle plate

- A patchwork foot of 9mm of grade number 47 or 47D
- A free-motion presser foot or a stitch regulator of grade number 42
- A free-hand motion quilt (e.g., the free-hand embroidery foot—grade number 24, or the ruler foot—grade number 96)
- Jeans needle of grade number 80
- Cotton thread
- A rotary cutting tool or scissors

**Instructions**

1. Start with four strips of lightly colored fabric and four other strips of darker color. Then, from each of the strips, cut out strips of length 7 inches

2. Attach the straight stitch needle plate, jeans needle, and the 9mm patchwork foot to the sewing machine to prepare it for piecing.

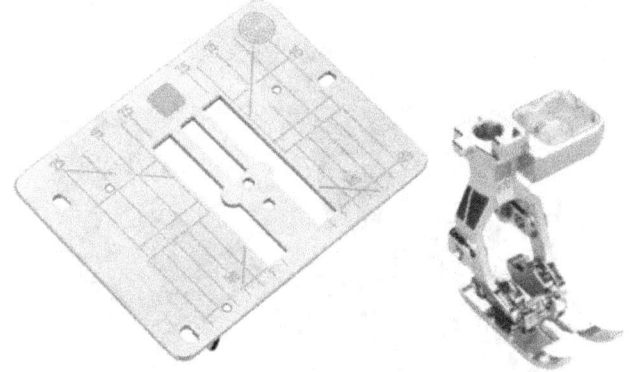

When you are done with the assembly, reduce the presser foot pressure by ten to fifteen units. Then, seam all three similar strips together.

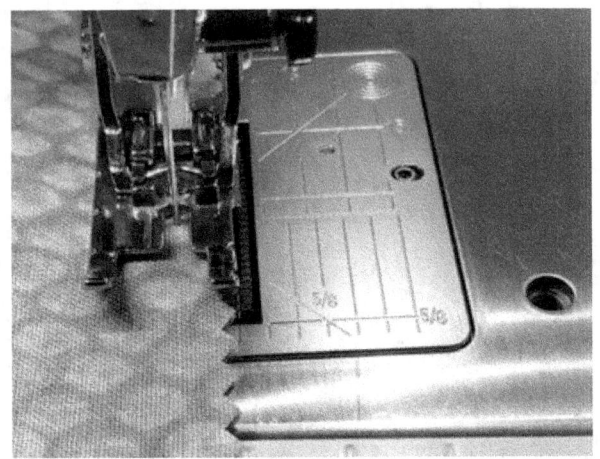

3. All seam allowances should be pressed in the same direction. Each of the sewed strips should be squared up to a 6 ½ inch block, totaling four light and four dark blocks.

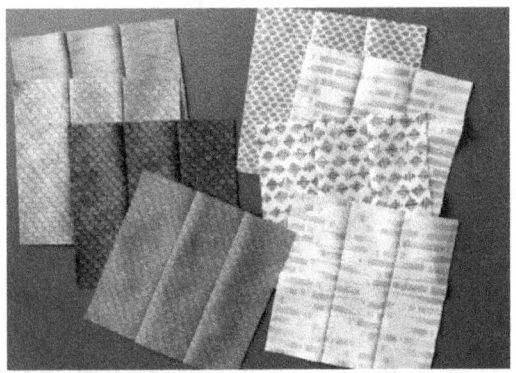

4. Sew the two blocks together with the dark square's seams running horizontally and the light square's seams running vertically.

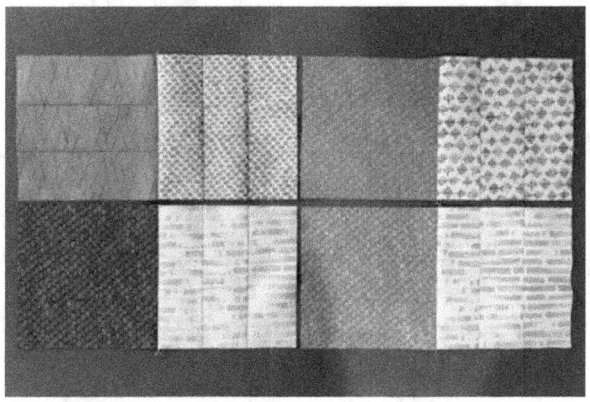

5. Measure the distance between the two blocks. They should be 12 ½" in length. Then, cut eight light strips to a length of 12 ½". As illustrated in the picture, sew the strips to the block sets.

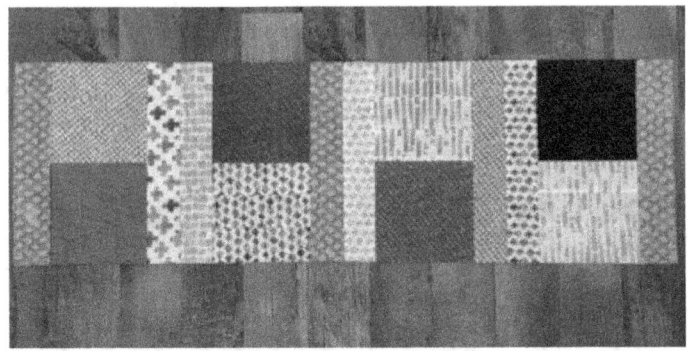

6. Baste the table runner after layering it with batting and backing.

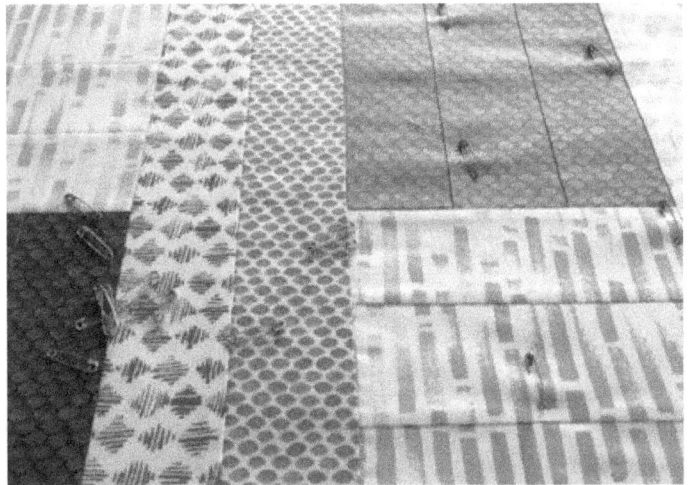

7. We'll use the blocks and strips to experiment with different free-motion fills. But, before we begin

working on the table runner, I'd like you to practice the fill with a pencil and paper.

The 6-inch dark square composed of the three strips will be quilted in a wavy plaid fill and worked as a solid square. Begin by sketching wavy lines on a sheet of paper big enough to accommodate several sketches, as shown below.

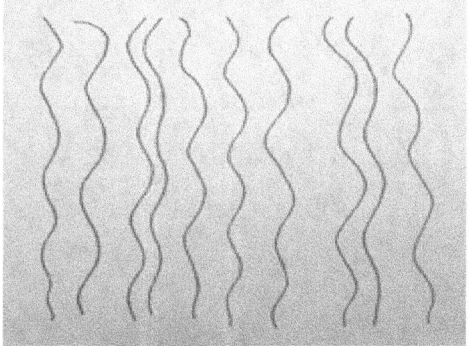

8. Now, cross the vertical lines with a set of horizontal wavy lines

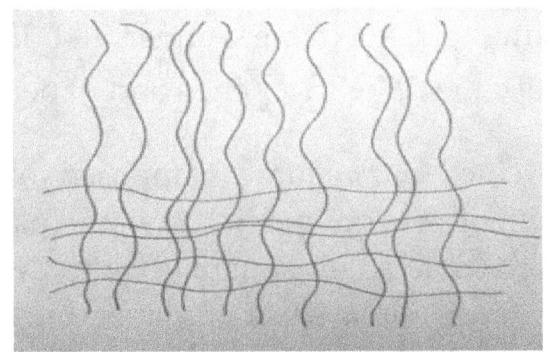

9. Proceed to the table runner's dark squares once you've gotten the hang of creating the design on paper. Insert a free-motion foot to your sewing machine and drop the feed dogs. When you start, pull up the bobbin thread. Sew the vertical lines together.

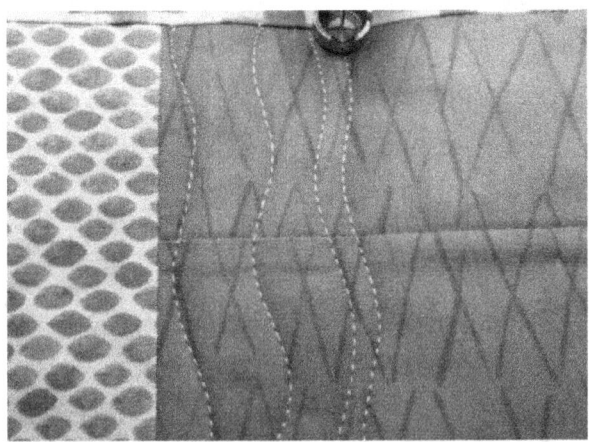

10. Stitch horizontal lines to fill the square upon using vertical lines to fill the square. You've completed the first wavy plaid fill.

11. The remaining fills for this table runner will be made in separate strips.

Let's proceed with the back and forth fill. Now, return to your sheet of paper, sketching lines 2 inches apart. Sketch a line from the first to the second line, then circle the corner and return to the first line. Proceed down the strip

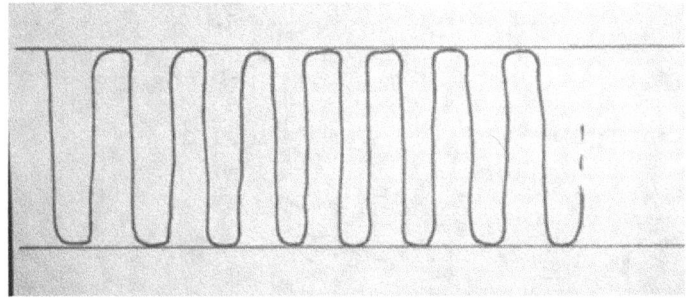

12. Make a stitch in one of the strips on the table runner.

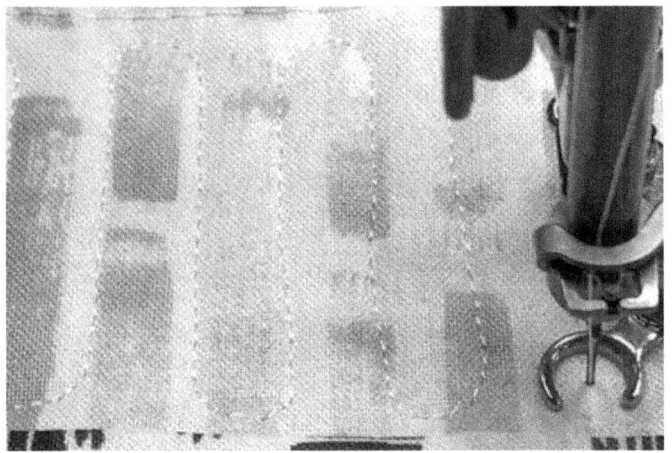

13. We'll utilize a similar action to construct the back and forth loop fill, given we've already constructed the back and forth fill earlier

Return to your sheet of paper once more. I will like to highlight the intended center of the loop since it's the first time making this fill. I've decided that my loops should be ¾-inches apart. Make a small mark ¾-inches from the paper's edge, then make subsequent ¾-inches marks across the bottom line. Place the first mark 3/8-inches from the edge on the top line, then ¾-inches apart. Sketch at an angle up to the right-hand side of the initial mark, starting around halfway between the 2 horizontal lines.

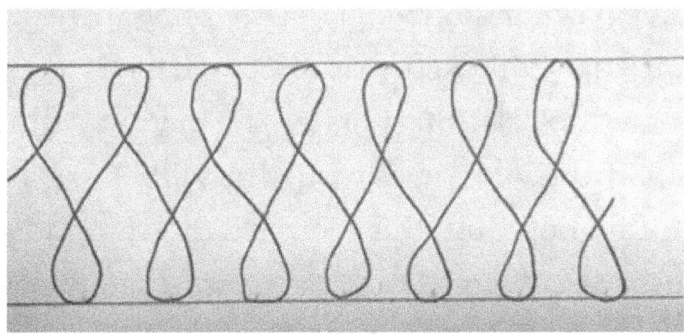

14. After getting the pattern right on paper, you can then move on to quilting it on specific strips of the table runner. This step is illustrated below

15. We'll expand on what you've previously done for our final fill. Return to your sheet of paper and draw spirals. Starting at the bottom, draw up, over, and down as you did with the back and forth Loops, but this loop this time around will be broader. Before changing direction to the left, don't go all the way down to the end. As represented by the arrows, continue in a spiral, going up, down, and over.

16. The pattern described above could be very tricky, so you should take your time to gain mastery of it before replicating it on your table runner. Run the stitches within the strips of the runner.

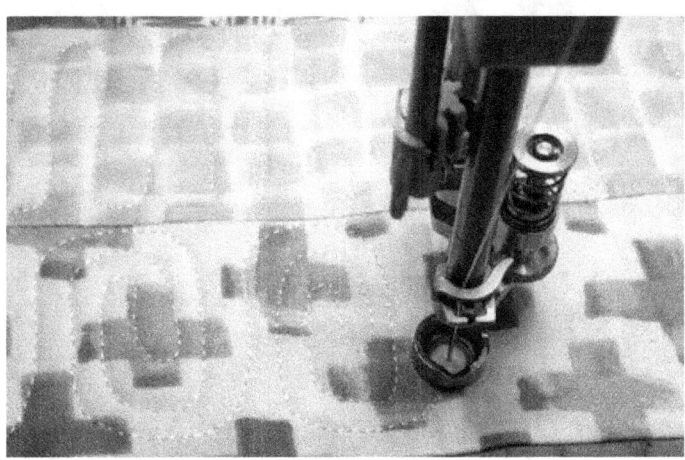

17. You're almost done with your runner. Keep in mind that the more you practice and quilt, the better you will get.

   Trim the runner's edges with a pair of scissors. Use varying lengths of 2 1/2" strips for the binding. End to end, sew them together with a 'mitered' seam until there is a minimum of 110" of fabric. Fold the runner in half and bind it.

## The End... Almost!

Hey! We've made it to the final chapter of this book, and I hope you've enjoyed it so far.

If you have not done so yet, I would be incredibly thankful if you could take just a minute to leave a quick review on Amazon

Reviews are not easy to come by, and as an independent author with a little marketing budget, I rely on you, my readers, to leave a short review on Amazon.

Even if it is just a sentence or two!

So if you really enjoyed this book, please...

>> Click here to leave a brief review on Amazon.

I truly appreciate your effort to leave your review, as it truly makes a huge difference.

# Chapter 6

# Troubleshooting Free-Motion Quilting Issues

You will encounter several challenges when you free-motion quilt, especially as a beginner. However, don't be frustrated by these challenges; they are normal and expected. With the quick fixes discussed below, you should be able to address the common problems encountered in this craft. So, let's get right into them.

**Unbalanced tension**

If the tension is unbalanced, loops or dots of thread will form on the upper and lower part of your quilt, which isn't particularly appealing.

Always practice on fabric and batting scraps before you pork on your quilt. Your tension will be fine if the stitches come out nice. If there are still loops or dots, you may need to alter your stitching speed (the rate your quilt moves through the machine) or tension.

To solve the issue of unbalanced tension, only modify the top tension for the latter above. If you have a tight top stitch(es) and the thread of the bobbin shows up on the front, relax it by reducing the tension number of the top thread. If you have a loose top stitch (es) with the top thread are appearing behind, tighten them by raising the tension number of the top thread.

To cover less-than-perfect tension, the same color thread in the top and bobbin can also be used.

**Thread breaking**

Nothing is more frustrating than getting halfway through a quilt and having a snapped thread or the bobbin running out.

When a thread snaps, take out as many stitches to make a hand knot with the two ends and tuck it into the batting. Return to where you left off quilting, and leave the tail ends loosened.

To avoid running out of bobbin, stitch as close to the quilt's edge as possible and keep an eye on your bobbin levels. When it becomes low, replace it with a new bobbin. You can utilize the remaining bobbin in your subsequent project or use it in practicing quilting on scraps

**Uneven quilting**

If your quilt does not hang properly or has wavy borders, it's likely that the quilting is unevenly distributed.

To solve this issue, use basic free-motion fillers such as pebbles, stippling, or loops to add more quilting to the background. Use a light thread of cotton with a neutral color if you do not want the extra quilting stitches to be visible.

**Unable to decide on a design**

Quilter's block is a terrible pain.

If you have finished your quilt sandwich but aren't sure what to sew across the top, snap your quilt top or design and print it out on an A4 paper. With a pen or pencil, sketch possible quilting designs on this paper.

Make a few copies so you can try out several quilting designs. After you're satisfied with an idea, quilt the idea on a different practice block before you apply it to the final quilt.

## Skipped stitches

There are a few causes that can result in stitches being skipped. Working through this list one item at a time is recommended.

- Is it necessary to replace the needle?
- Is the needle sticky from stitching through applique work, for example? If this is the case, turn the machine off, detach the needle, and wipe it clean with nail varnish remover. Replace the needle, turn on the device, and try once more.
- Are the stitches coming together? It's possible that the needle thread isn't always connecting with the bobbin thread to complete the stitch. Adjust the darning foot to sit a little lower if it's adjustable, and try to stitch again. Before continuing, do the latter a few times to be sure this isn't the issue.
- Is the needle in the machine properly positioned? Needles are prone to slipping. With time,

your needles could slip downward. Remove and replace the needle after turning off the machine.
- Do you have matching threads? The needle and bobbin threads should have similar thickness or weight for the threads to match. To see if this is the issue, wind a bobbin of the top thread and use it to check if the issue with skipped stitches continues

## Loose stitches

Threading issues are nearly always the cause of loose stitches. Remove all top and bottom threads and carefully rethread, ensuring that the presser foot is up while threading the top thread and the bobbin thread is threaded via the tension guide of the bobbin thread.

Mismatched threads are another cause of loose stitches. To see if mismatched threads are the problem, use the same procedure as before.

## Puckering fabric

Threading issues or a fabric that isn't stable or thick enough to keep the stitches firmly might cause puckering. See suggestions given above for the thread.

For added support and stability, add a few stitches and tear paper stabilizers beneath the fabric. Lastly, ensure the needle you're using is razor-sharp.

# Conclusion

At this point, you should have a sheet of paper or a workbook with sketches of the designs you will likely want to quilt on your fabric, but first, practice, practice, practice before implementation – this will make you feel very confident in quilting your free-motion project. Overall, ensure you are relaxed as much as possible! Free-motion quilting involves the movement of most parts of your body. If you are tensed or worked up while quilting, it will reflect awfully in your quilts. Ensure you have a good grapse of the chapters covered in this book before making your first project. Mistakes will be made along the way; however, I know it will turn out as expected eventually.

Happy quilting, quilters!

www.ingramcontent.com/pod-product-compliance
Lightning Source LLC
Chambersburg PA
CBHW071419070526
44578CB00003B/613